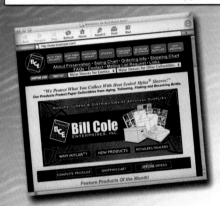
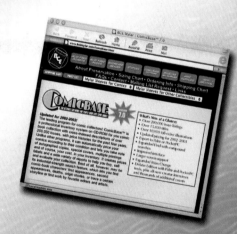
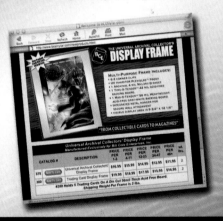

CGC Offers the Most Services in the

Steve Borock   *Mark Haspel*   *Paul Litch*

CGC Offers the Most Trusted Grading

CGC maintains a steadfast commitment to a standard of consistent and accurate grading. Our grading team is made up of the most experienced and widely recognized experts in the field.

CGC Has the Most Innovative Holder

The innovative holder design is the most reliable means of safe storage for your comic books. Through extensive research and development we feel the CGC holder provides the most effective barrier from harmful elements.

CGC Holds the Most Respected Endorsements

"CGC has made the grading debate at conventions disappear. As a dealer in the high-end market, I no longer spend hours debating on who's the better grader, because CGC has now set the industry standard."

Bob Storms • Highgradecomics.com

"So far CGC has shown integrity, good intentions, and above all, the desire to improve by listening to the people they serve."

Matt Nelson • Classic Conservation

"I am going to keep purchasing via mailorder and let CGC do my grading for me. Let me tell you mate, I have been burnt more than once in the past with overgraded and restored books. CGC is a godsend in that regard-thanks for your efforts."

Ben Teoh • Collector (Australia)

"I could go on and on about why I like Comics Guaranty, but the bottom line is that they are going to make this hobby a lot safer and a lot more fun."

Mike Grissmer • Collector

"The last 6 months the level of commitment to customer service and turnaround on graded comics has surpassed all of my expectations. The future of comic book collecting is CGC."

Vincent Zurzolo • Metropolis

"The level of accuracy, consistency, professionalism and beauty of the end product at CGC has revolutionized, energized and stabilized this hobby, lifting it to a height that would have otherwise been impossible."

Mark Wilson • PGC Mint

For information on submitting your comic books call us or visit our website at CGCcomics.com!

4

Comprehensive Set of Comic Book Hobby

CGC Presents the CGC Census Report

The CGC Census Report is the only tool of its kind, and allows CGC customers to visit our website www.CGCcomics.com, click on "Census", and search through the many thousands of comic books CGC has certified to date.

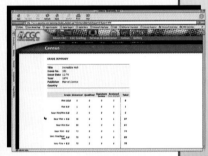

This revolutionary and invaluable tool enables buyers and sellers to better understand the rarity of the grade of each comic book they are buying and selling, so they have all the data at their fingertips to make informed decisions. The census will be updated no less than every quarter and is completely free.

Chris Friesen

CGC Provides Restoration Check

Part of the CGC grading team's review of your comic book is to perform a thorough restoration check. When detected, restoration is noted on the purple grading label. This restoration check is included in the grading fee whereas a restoration check elsewhere may cost up to $100.

IT'S FREE!

Auction Prices
Here, we'll let you know everything that's happening in the auction world - from upcoming shows to results of recent shows to profiles of the biggest items up for grabs.

Industry News
This section will fill you in on all the important goings-on in the comic and collecting industries.

Superstars
In this section, we'll focus on the people making news. Birthdays, anniversaries, promotions, weddings . . . if it has a human interest, we'll highlight it here.

The Main Event
This is where you'll find your new feature articles. These are the lead stories that get to the heart of current trends and sizzling news.

Catch the Wave
Here we'll focus on new products that any savvy collector would find of interest.

Did You Know...?
This is the section for the lover of nostalgia - particularly obscure nostalgia. We'll report on the toys, characters, & clubs that are finally regaining popularity.

In the Limelight
In this section, we'll give an in-depth profile of a Star Collector.

Mondo Media
Here we'll give you up-to-the-minute box-office wrap-ups, trivia, and features from the movie, TV, radio and journalism worlds.

Off the Presses
If you're looking to find the best in new reference books and publications of all sorts, we'll give you the lowdown here.

Savvy Sites
These are the sites we find interesting, and chances are you will too!

Did you get the SCOOP?
an e-mail newsletter

It's new. It's free. It's all the news you'll click to print.™

Be among the first to receive Scoop, the most comprehensive source of information for collectors and pop culture enthusiasts of all ages, sponsored by Diamond International Galleries and Gemstone Publishing, Inc.

e-mail Jaime Bramble at bjaime@gemstonepub.com to sign up or visit scoop.diamondgalleries.com

Do you have a question about a collectible you'd like to see us answer? E-mail John Snyder at sjohn@diamondgalleries.com!

OFFICIAL overstreet
COMIC BOOK
grading
guide Second Edition

COVERING CERTIFIED AND NON-CERTIFIED COMICS
FULLY ILLUSTRATED WITH A COMPLETE GLOSSARY

by ROBERT M. OVERSTREET & ARNOLD T. BLUMBERG

GEMSTONE PUBLISHING

J.C. Vaughn, **Executive Editor**
Arnold T. Blumberg, **Editor** • Brenda Busick, **Creative Director**
Mark Huesman, **Pricing Coordinator**
Jamie David, **Office Manager**
Jaime Bramble, **Editorial Coordinator**

SPECIAL CONTRIBUTORS TO THIS EDITION

Steve Borock • Susan Cicconi-Killiany • Russ Cochran • Tom Gordon • Bruce Hamilton
Denis Kitchen • Dale Moore • Marc Nathan • Matt Nelson • Chuck Rozanski • J.C. Vaughn

SENIOR OVERSTREET ADVISORS FOR OVER 25 YEARS

Dave Alexander • Bruce Hamilton • Paul Levitz • Michelle Nolan
Terry Stroud • Harry B. Thomas • Doug Sulipa • Raymond S. True

SENIOR OVERSTREET ADVISORS FOR OVER 20 YEARS

Gary M. Carter • Bill Cole • Gene Seger • Steve Geppi • Stan Gold
M. Thomas Inge • Phil Levine • Richard Olson • Ron Pussell
David R. Smith • John K. Snyder Jr.

SPECIAL ADVISORS

Dave Anderson • David J. Anderson, D.D.S. • Robert L. Beerbohm • Jon Berk • Steve Borock
John Chruscinski • Gary Colabuono • Larry Curcio • Gary Dolgoff • Joe Dungan • Conrad Eschenberg
Richard Evans • Stephen Fishler • Philip J. Gaudino • Steve Gentner • Michael Goldman • Jamie Graham
Daniel Greenhalgh • Eric Groves • Gary Guzzo • John Grasse • Jim Halperin • Mark Haspel • John Hauser
John Hone • George Huang • Bill Hughes • Rob Hughes • Ed Jaster • Joseph Koch • Joe Mannarino
Rick Manzella • Harry Matetsky • Jon McClure • Matt Nelson • Michael Naiman • Josh Nathanson
James Payette • John Petty • Yolanda Ramirez • Todd Reznik • "Doc" Robinson • Robert Rogovin • Rory Root
Robert Roter • Chuck Rozanski • Matt Schiffman • Dave Smith • Laura Sperber • Tony Starks • Joel Thingvall
Joe Vereneault • Frank Verzyl • John Verzyl • Rose Verzyl • Jerry Weist • Harley Yee • Vincent Zurzolo, Jr.

The Crown Publishing Group
New York   Gemstone Publishing

THE OFFICIAL OVERSTREET COMIC BOOK GRADING GUIDE Copyright © 1992, 2002 by Gemstone Publishing, Inc. All rights reserved. Printed in the United States of America. No part of this book may be used or reproduced in any manner whatsoever without written permission except in the case of brief quotations embodied in critical articles and reviews. For information, write to: Gemstone Publishing, 1966 Greenspring Drive, Suite LL3, Timonium, Maryland 21093.

Gemstone Publishing Edition: Cover art: The Incredible Hulk #181 ©2002 Marvel Characters, Inc. All rights reserved. Random House edition – Wolverine #1 ©2002 Marvel Characters, Inc.; Amazing Spider-Man #1 ©2002 Marvel Characters, Inc.; Detective Comics #27 ©2002 DC Comics; Captain Marvel Jr. #1 ©2002 DC Comics; All-Flash Quarterly #1 ©2002 DC Comics; G.I. Joe #1 ©2002 Hasbro.

THE OFFICIAL OVERSTREET COMIC BOOK GRADING GUIDE (2nd Edition) is an original publication of Gemstone Publishing, Inc. and House of Collectibles. Distributed by The Crown Publishing Group, a division of Random House, Inc., New York and simultaneously in Canada by Random House of Canada Limited, Toronto. This edition has never before appeared in book form.

House of Collectibles
The Crown Publishing Group
299 Park Ave.
New York, New York 10171

www.houseofcollectibles.com

Overstreet is a registered trademark of Gemstone Publishing, Inc.

 House of Collectibles is a registered trademark and the H colophon is a trademark of Random House, Inc.

Published by arrangement with Gemstone Publishing.

ISBN: 0-609-81052-9 (Random House edition)

Printed in the United States of America

10 9 8 7 6 5 4 3 2 1

Second Edition: January 2003

Table of Contents

Acknowledgements

This kind of book simply can't be made in a vacuum. Without the guidance and support of many informed individuals throughout the comic book collecting community who lent their time and expertise during the production of this book, we would never have been able to complete the volume you now hold in your hands. This book is a tribute to the cohesive efforts of everyone involved.

Thanks to all the Overstreet advisors, comic book dealers, collectors and other enthusiasts who offered their time and expertise to advise on matters of grading: Dave Anderson, Jon Berk, Gary Colabuono, Gary Dolgoff, Steven R. Eichenbaum, Stephen Gentner, Stephen A. Geppi, Tom Gordon, Eric Groves, Tracey Heft, Jef Hinds, Bill Hughes, Michael McKenzie, Dale Moore, Michael Naiman, Jim Payette, Yolanda Ramirez, Marnin Rosenberg, Matt Schiffman, John K. Snyder Jr., Doug Sulipa, Michael Tierney, and Jon Verzyl.

Special thanks of course to all of our contributors: Steve Borock, Susan Cicconi-Killiany, Russ Cochran, Tom Gordon, Bruce Hamilton, Denis Kitchen, Dale Moore, Marc Nathan, Matt Nelson, Chuck Rozanski, and J.C. Vaughn.

Special thanks as well to Gary M. Carter, who contributed so much to the first edition of this book, and to whom a continuing "huzzah" is owed for his efforts.

To the many others who offered advice and/or support through letter and e-mail, including but not limited to: Ken Applequist, Kathy Bates, Mike Benson, Jim Brocius, John Chaney, John Cimisi, Kim Cook, Lynda Crabtree, Frank Daniels, Vince D'Augelli, Tim Gray, Charlie Harris, Garth Holmes, James Holtz, John Hutchins, Daniel Imbierowski, Dave Karchner, Michael Larsen, Donna Magers, Pramodh Munbodh, Sam Papale, Mike and Arlene Parks, "Bear" Payne, Jeff Rabkin, Erik Roggenburg, Mike Rozmus, Ellie Schellhase, Bob Shippee, Gerry Sorek, Trevor Stamper, Boyd and Dallas Stephens, Michael Sullivan, Bill Turner, Jerome Wenker, Doug Wheeler, Gary Woloszyn, and Bill Yawien.

Thanks must also go to the good folks at the eBay "Comics-O-Rama" discussion board, including (but not limited to): Sean Budde, Morris Berndt, Raphael Cheli, Daniel Eng, Paul Ference, Nick Pope, Gary Reitmeyer, James Ashley Rudd, Lance Shoeman (loved the ODOR card!), Bob Turner, and Joseph Vonheeder.

If we've forgotten anybody, we apologize for the omission, but acknowledge gratefully the contributions of anyone who took the time to offer their guidance and express their thoughts on grading as we compiled this volume.

Special credit is due the ever-diligent and talented production staff of Gemstone Publishing for their tireless efforts in creating a new full-color book from scratch: Brenda Busick (Creative Director), Mark Huesman (Pricing Coordinator - layout man extraordinaire), Jamie David (Office Manager), and Jaime Bramble (Editorial Coordinator), as well as to our Executive Editor, J.C. Vaughn - he knows his "odd formats!" - for their invaluable contributions to this guide.

Thanks to Joe McGuckin and Mike Wilbur for photographic and research support.

Bob would like to thank his wife, Caroline, for her encouragement and support on such a tremendous project. Arnold would like to thank his parents, Marvin and Rochelle, who – when he told them he'd have to buy replacement copies of some '70s Marvel comics once he realized what putting name stickers on the covers had done to their condition – never once suggested he was crazy...or at least, wisely kept it to themselves.

Finally, our thanks to all who placed advertisements in this book.

Foreword
by Chuck Rozanski

As the owner of the largest back issue comics company in America, with over 32 years of experience buying and selling vintage comic books, I have had to oversee the grading of approximately 20 million comics. In most instances, this has been a very easy job, as my staff sorts through thousands of recent, and relatively inexpensive, comics each day. Since most of those issues easily fall into the VF and NM categories, it is only the occasional flawed copy that causes any measure of real scrutiny.

Where the job becomes much more difficult is when comics become expensive and/or date from prior to 1980. Then grading becomes a subjective exercise in which your overall optimism has to be severely tempered by the harsh reality that all defects present in a given book must be fairly taken into account, and an ultimate grade be arrived at that satisfies not only your need as a dealer to derive the highest possible revenue from the book, but also the customer's right to receive a book which clearly meets all the criteria of the assigned grade. This becomes particularly important when a given comic book has a current value that is in the thousands, or tens of thousands, of dollars.

Where this book has great value to the hobby of comics collecting is in its unbiased and objective presentation of standards that have been generally agreed to by the vast majority of the comics collecting community. For over 30 years, Bob Overstreet has been universally accepted as the arbiter of prices and grading within the comics collecting world. He has recently worked with his staff to update his orig-inal 1992 grading guide to not only clarify specific grading issues, but also to revise the standards to meet the market conditions of 2002. This is a critical distinction to draw, as the comics collecting world is in a continual state of evolutionary flux, and grading standards evolve as new dealers and collectors have their views integrated into the overall standards by which comics are graded. The recent introduction of third-party grading has also caused significant changes in how extremely high grade comics are evaluated, as the pricing multiples awarded to books in the 9.6 and higher categories have led to an unprecedented level of scrutiny on comics that are represented to be in Near Mint+ and higher grades.

As an individual comics dealer, I find that I can readily endorse the grading definitions arrived upon by the Gemstone staff in this book. They are somewhat more stringent than those we all employed in 1992, but I believe that they also accurately represent the current mindset of most comics dealers and collectors. With this new book in hand, we now have a set of criteria under which we can all enjoy buying and selling comics with a minimum of uncertainty as to the accuracy of grading on any given issue.

With that having been said, please note that I don't believe that this book, or any book, could ever remove all doubts about the grading of any comic book. Grading comics involves such an extraordinary number of subjective analyses that it is literally impossible to devise a system that could take into account the myriad of potential flaws that might appear in any given book. Unlike coins, stamps, and cards which

Chuck Rozanski has been the owner and president of Mile High Comics, Inc. since 1969. Known throughout the comics world for his discovery of the legendary Mile High/Edgar Church collection of Mint Golden Age comics, Chuck lives today on his organic vegetable farm in Boulder, Colorado with his wife of 25 years, Nanette, and daughters Rowan (22), Aleta (19), Tanith (17), and Elsbeth (15).

are small and relatively easy to grade, comics are so large and complex in their potential for minor defects that it is always a struggle to evaluate how to weigh the individual physical characteristics of any given book so as to arrive at a reasonable grade. That's exactly what makes this book so valuable to anyone considering purchasing collectible comics, as it covers the vast majority of readily identifiable characteristics of grading, and minimizes the areas in which a subjective definition has to be generated. Quite literally, if you are a comics collector working without this book, you are flying blind. You might be grading correctly as defined by the standards of your local area, but do you really know the national standards? Thanks to the team at Gemstone Publishing, you now can have that knowledge in the palm of your hand.

In closing, I would like to say that I had more than a little trepidation about endorsing this new edition of **The Official Overstreet Comic Book Grading Guide**. There has been much controversy during the past year about the degree to which grading standards have changed within the comics collecting community during the past decade. I have been very vocal in my opposition to an extreme tightening of standards, and have worked hard to be sure that a middle ground was reached between all parties involved in the controversy. It pleases me very much that the Gemstone staff, after taking into account the input from thousands of collectors and dealers, arrived at a set of standards which are a very reasonable reflection of the current state of comic book grading. Once again, the leadership of Bob Overstreet has been instrumental in resolving a dispute which was distracting many of us from our enjoyment of the comics collecting hobby. My hat is off to Bob, and his hardworking staff, for creating an excellent encore edition of his original grading guide.

Chuck Rozanski,
President - Mile High Comics, Inc.
September, 2002

Preface
by Bruce Hamilton

J uan Ponce de Leon, the Spanish explorer, sought the perfect life and searched Florida for the "Fountain of Youth." He failed to find it, of course.

Throughout history, man's frustrating quest for perfection has woven through all facets of his life, blanketing his work, his play, and his dreams. The teenage boy lusts for a nubile, perfect "10" girl; churches fill with parishioners looking for a pathway to heaven; peddlers hope to win salesman-of-the-year awards; the housewife shops for fruit with no bruises; Olympians train for years to set best-ever records; the wealthy spend thousands on a watch that tells time no better than a $39.95 model; students stay up all night cramming for an examination, hoping to score a perfect 100.

Collectors, too, have been searching for perfection since collecting began, looking for their treasures from antiquity, hoping to find them in Mint, like-new condition. But what is Mint? How is a collector to know it when he sees it? Is it possible to arrive at a formula to know what to pay for Mint or does it justify whatever you can afford? Bob Overstreet's new Grading Guide will, I think, fill your head with new perspectives on the hobby and should help you to come to some of your own answers to these perplexing questions.

It's been fascinating over the years to watch the definition of Mint change in the comic book marketplace. In the 1960s, comics were either collectible or uncollectible, and the condition most dealers were satisfied to describe was "good or better." I asked pioneer Phil Seuling why he didn't specify the condition of his comic books in more detail. His response was, "What do you expect me to do? Sit down and grade every one? I've got thousands. It would take days." Mint was a coin-dealer's term he didn't think should apply to comic books. But there were already collectors and a few dealers who thought differently.

Fans would rifle through newsstand racks in those days to pick out the best copies and say, "Ah, these are surely Mint!" They began to seek older books that looked like new ones. For every collector who wanted Mint comics and was willing to pay more to obtain that rare, elusive "perfect" condition, a dealer would pop up to obligingly help him find them. And, not surprisingly, debates began.

Collectors started to compare comics, soon concluding that if they had two Mint comic books and one was better, then one was not Mint. This is to presuppose the position that Mint means perfect, better than like new: An unattainable goal. Is this what collectors should seek - the impossible? I think not. It only seems reasonable that the best available, the best possible, should be the goal. Then, one questions, why not call that Mint?

Conscientious dealers - and I believe I was one of them - steadfastly refused to grade anything above Near Mint. I remember with irony a time when I sold copies from one of the legendary top-grade collections in the 1970s, the best of which I described as only "Near Mint." There was a collector from the Midwest named Pennack, who had a reputation for fussiness in his quest for Mint comic books: Dealers who

---

Bruce Hamilton is a leading collector, historian and publisher in the field of comic character collectibles, particularly in the arena of Disney-themed items. In addition to authoring numerous articles and contributing to price guides and other publications, he has published comics, and produced lithographs, figurines and other high quality collectibles. He is one of the foremost authorities on the life and works of Carl Barks.

sold to him coined the phrase "Pennack perfect" to describe what he would buy. Pennack wouldn't respond to my ads offering "Near Mint," but a Texas dealer did buy from me and resold the same comics to Pennack, who later touted them as being some of the choicest in his collection. It was a sobering experience.

Chaos is the natural order of things, including the deterioration of comic books. Deterioration begins immediately after printing and continues through binding, distribution, selling, handling, reading, and eventually by just keeping, aging in the passage of time. If all comic books were in perfect condition and remained that way - impervious to damage - would the old ones be worth anything today? Would the hobby itself, in fact, even exist? Is it not true, after all, that those things we value most are only temporal or fragile: A flower, a sunset, a perfect day, life itself...or a Mint comic book?

How great it would be, a chorus of voices will likely shout, if all comics were perfect and prices thereby remained low! We would all be able to afford to go out and buy, cheaply, what we wanted. "Oh, happy day!" as Johnny Mercer penned in the lyrics to the musical, *Li'l Abner*. But the real world doesn't work that way. There would be no dealers to seek them out to sell and, alas, I'm afraid by this time, most would have already been thrown away by their original owners.

As life isn't perfect, there are absolutely no perfect comic books. So, is a grading guide needed? The answer is yes. The new grading range of 9.9-10.0 can and should be termed Mint. The best copies known of vintage comics should have a top classification, and somehow "Near Mint" doesn't cut it. As far as the term has become generic, and despite the fact that coins are minted, stamps and comics are printed and automobiles are manufactured, everybody understands when you call perfect examples Mint. Let's put the issue to rest.

Grading standards have continued to evolve after the appearance of Overstreet's first grading guide over ten years ago. New grading terms have been in wide use throughout the industry as well as the conversion of the old 100 point system to a much simpler 10 point system three years ago. Values of vintage comic books have climbed into six figures making accurate grading more important than ever. Congratulations to Bob Overstreet and his staff for putting together this landmark 2nd edition!

Bruce Hamilton,
September, 2002

19

24

25

BUYING ALL COMICS

with 10 and 12¢ cover prices

TOP PRICES PAID!

IMMEDIATE CASH PAYMENT

Stop Throwing Away Those Old Comic Books!

I'm always paying top dollar for any pre-1966 comic. No matter what title or condition, whether you have one comic or a warehouse full.

Get my bid, you'll be glad you did!

I will travel anywhere to view large collections, or you may box them up and send for an expert appraisal and immediate payment of my top dollar offer. Satisfaction guaranteed.

For a quick reply Send a List of What You Have or Call Toll Free

1-800-791-3037

or

1-608-277-8750

or write

Jef Hinds
P.O. Box 44803
Madison, WI 53744-4803

Also available for
Insurance & Estate Appraisals, Strictly Confidential.

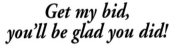

Human Torch, All Winners, Spider-Man, Captain America © Marvel, All Star, Batman, Superman © DC

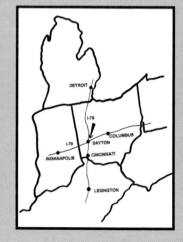

THE DEFINITIVE VISUAL GUIDE AND CHECKLIST!

Gemstone Publishing is proud to present the Fourth Edition of the book the **Maine Antique Digest** called "...without a doubt the most informative price guide written." **Hake's Price Guide To Character Toys** is "The Definitive Visual Price Guide & Checklist,"™ - a veritable phonebook full of toy treasures from the past century right up through this year. Don't you know a fellow collector who would love this book?

Hake #1

Hake #2

Hake #3

First Edition - $24.95
Second Edition - $24.95
Third Edition $35.00

You can also get the historic previous editions of **Hake's Price Guide** for your collection. These remarkable volumes unfold the story of comic character collectibles before your eyes. Don't miss out as they become collector's items themselves!

Also available as sets!
Set A: Hake's Price Guide #1, 2 & 3 - $75.00 (regularly $84.90)
Set B: Hake's Price Guide #1, 2, 3 & 4 - $100 (regularly $119.90)
Prices do not include shipping & handling.

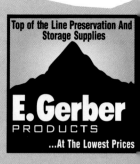

GePPi'S
COMIC WORLD

1116 N. Rolling Road
Baltimore, MD 21228
(410) 788-0900

Comics, Games, Statues,
Storage Supplies,
Mini-busts, Lunch Boxes,
Magazines & More!

▼

New and Back Issues

▼

Special Orders,
Hardcovers,
Trade Paperbacks

▼

Buying & Selling

▼

Subscription Service

43

47

AN ANNUAL EVENT!

Since 1970, every year
The Overstreet Comic Book Price Guide
debuts with the latest prices, market reports and insights
into the history and future of comics and collecting!
If you're serious about comics, there's only one
book for you!

48

49

"FAR AS I'M CONCERNED, THE REAL SUPERHEROES ARE THOSE GREAT GUYS AT HERITAGE. I REALLY LUCKED OUT WHEN I MET 'EM 'CAUSE THEY GOT ME PRICES THAT EXCEEDED MY WILDEST EXPECTATIONS, PLUS IT WAS A REAL KICK TO WORK WITH THEM. I DON'T WANT THIS TO SOUND LIKE A TV COMMERCIAL BUT, SO HELP ME SPIDEY, THERE'S NO ONE I'D RATHER ENTRUST WITH MY COLLECTION. EXCELSIOR!"

—STAN LEE, CO-CREATOR OF SPIDER-MAN, THE FANTASTIC FOUR, THE X-MEN...

"JOHN PETTY AND THE STAFF AT HERITAGE COMICS ARE AMONG THE MOST PROFESSIONAL PEOPLE I HAVE EVER DEALT WITH. WHILE THEIR KNOWLEDGE AND EXPERTISE IN THE FIELD OF COLLECTING IS BEYOND REPROACH, IT IS THEIR ABILITY TO MAKE YOU FEEL LIKE A FRIEND AND NOT JUST A CLIENT THAT STEPS THEM AHEAD OF MOST OTHER AUCTIONEERS."

—JOE JUSKO, ARTIST / PAINTER

"ANOTHER SUPER AUCTION! AS A CONSIGNOR, I AM VERY PLEASED WITH THE RESULTS."

—RUSS COCHRAN,
AUTHOR, PUBLISHER, AND COMICS HISTORIAN

"IN MY LONG EXPERIENCE IN THIS BUSINESS, I'VE NEVER SEEN SUCH AN ATMOSPHERE OF PROFESSION-ALISM AND TEAMWORK AS DEMONSTRATED BY THE HERITAGE GROUP. I WAS PRESENT AT EACH OF THE AUCTION SESSIONS AND IT WAS ENERGIZING TO SEE JIM HALPERIN NOT ONLY ATTENDING BUT TAKING AN ACTIVE ROLE. IT'S NOT UNUSUAL FOR THE TOP PEOPLE IN AN AUCTION FIRM TO NOT ATTEND THE ACTUAL EVENTS, BUT JIM WAS INVOLVED, ENTHUSIASTIC AND EFFECTIVE. HIS TEAM REFLECTED HIS COMMITMENT. IT WAS AN EXCEPTIONAL BIT OF HISTORY."

—JOHN SNYDER,
PRESIDENT OF DIAMOND INTERNATIONAL GALLERIES

"THE TEAM AT HERITAGE DID A GREAT JOB ON THE JULY SIGNATURE AUCTION. THEY GOT THE WORD OUT, INCREASED THE GENERAL PUBLIC'S AWARENESS OF THE VALUE OF COLLECTIBLE COMICS, AND RAISED THE BAR FOR THOSE OF US IN THE INDUSTRY. I'M LOOKING FORWARD TO CONTINUING OUR RELATIONSHIP WITH HERITAGE FOR A VERY LONG TIME."

—STEVE GEPPI, OWNER AND FOUNDER OF DIAMOND COMIC DISTRIBUTORS

RUSS COCHRAN'S
COMIC ART
A U C T I O N

Russ Cochran's Comic Art Auction

started in 1973 with the publication of his illustrated art catalog, Graphic Gallery. Soon after that, it became the main source of comic strip and comic book art, as well as paintings by Carl Barks and Frank Frazetta. It is safe to say that Russ Cochran sold more Barks and Frazetta paintings than all the other dealers in comic art combined.

At the same time, auctions were being held for the EC original art, all of which passed through Russ's Comic Art Auction. Dozens of important originals by Hal Foster, Alex Raymond, George Herriman, George McManus, Milton Caniff, and virtually every comic artist have passed through the pages of this auction catalog, finding their way to comic art collections all over the western world.

In all, a total of 13 issues of Graphic Gallery were published, and to date, 63 issues of the Comic Art Auction.

If you are a collector of comic art, or if you have art to consign, contact

Russ Cochran at
1-800-EC CRYPT, or at
russcochran@townsqr.com

**BUYING OLD COMICS AND RELATED ITEMS
MADE BETWEEN 1930-1975.**

**LHCOMICS@LYCOS.COM
LEROY HARPER
P.O. BOX 63
CLINTON, KY 42031
270-653-5118**

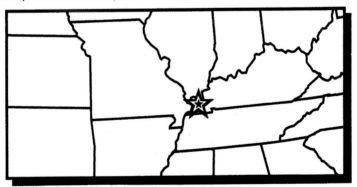

DID YOU KNOW?

...Hoppyland?
What California theme park opened its doors to hoards of screaming, happy children on May 27, 1951? If you said Disneyland, you're wrong! It was actually Hoppyland, a theme park devoted to all things Hopalong Cassidy.

...Yellow Submarine?
You know how the song goes. But, did you know that when the film *Yellow Submarine* was released, there were two different versions of the movie poster?

...Silver Surfer?
Bowen Designs recently released an extremely-limited-edition variant version of their popular Silver Surfer mini-bust, available only to attendees of Wizard World 2002 in Chicago.

...Mickey Mouse's 75th Birthday?
Did you know that next year will mark 75 years since a little mouse called Mickey first scurried onto the scene in 1928?

...Valric of the Vikings?
In 1941, all you had to do to get your Viking Magnifying ring was send your All-Rye Flakes box top to Kellogg's, along with a modest 10 cents. Soon you'd be the proud owner of what is now one of the most rare and valuable of collectible toy rings.

...Squirt Guns?
Did you know that back in the day, squirt guns could be clipped around the handlebars of any bicycle, or even tricycle, for a whole breed of fun that a silly old horn just couldn't provide?

...Og the Cave Boy?
It's a common belief that the stories of cave-boy adventurer Og were exclusively limited to radio, but did you know they actually began appearing as early as 1921?

...Basil Wolverton?
He never had a single art lesson, but he's been called "the Hieronymous Bosch of comics." He's also been called "the most bizarre cartoonist who ever lived." And though he was one of the greatest artists of the Golden Age, Basil Wolverton is also well known for a completely different kind of illustration. Yes, the man best known for his creepy space freaks and grossly out-of-proportion weirdos made a whole new name for himself in 1961 with his work on *The Bible Story*.

...One Man's Family?
Did you know that the longest running serial drama in the history of radio was a heartwarming tale of life and love called *One Man's Family*?

an e-mail newsletter

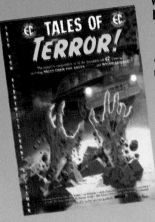

RUSS COCHRAN'S
COMIC ART
A U C T I O N

Russ Cochran's Comic Art Auction

started in 1973 with the publication of his illustrated art catalog, Graphic Gallery. Soon after that, it became the main source of comic strip and comic book art, as well as paintings by Carl Barks and Frank Frazetta. It is safe to say that Russ Cochran sold more Barks and Frazetta paintings than all the other dealers in comic art combined.

At the same time, auctions were being held for the EC original art, all of which passed through Russ's Comic Art Auction. Dozens of important originals by Hal Foster, Alex Raymond, George Herriman, George McManus, Milton Caniff, and virtually every comic artist have passed through the pages of this auction catalog, finding their way to comic art collections all over the western world.

In all, a total of 13 issues of Graphic Gallery were published, and to date, 63 issues of the Comic Art Auction.

If you are a collector of comic art, or if you have art to consign, contact

Russ Cochran at
1-800-EC CRYPT, or at
russcochran@townsqr.com

Where the Super-Heroes are Found!

JACK KIRBY

Jay Parrino's The Mint

Post Office Drawer 9326 • Kansas City, MO 64133
JayParrino.com • whughes199@yahoo.com
(972) 691-8837 Fax

(866) 355-4591

© Marvel

THE COMIC ART PRICE GUIDE

Second Edition
With Pulp, U.G. Comix, and Monster Magazine Price Guides

Jerry Weist

EXPLORE THE HISTORY OF COMIC ART IN THE COMIC ART PRICE GUIDE!

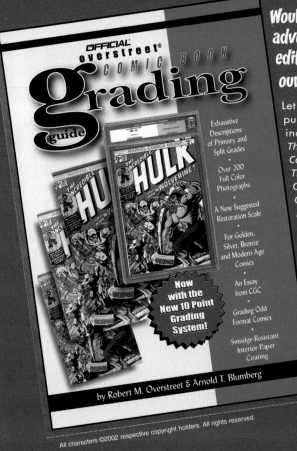

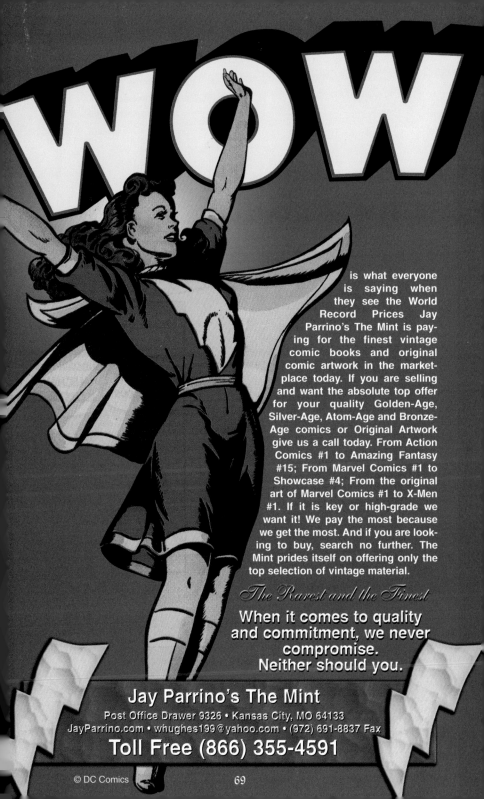

Business Card Ads

Shop Directory

You can have your store listed here for very reasonable rates. Send for details for next year's Guide. The following list of stores have paid to be included in this list. We cannot assume any responsibility in your dealings with these shops. This list is provided for your information only. When planning trips, it would be advisable to make appointments in advance. Remember, to get your shop included in the next edition, contact us for rates. **Gemstone Publishing, Inc., 1966 Greenspring Dr., Suite LL3, Timonium, MD 21093. PH 888-375-9800 or 410-560-5806, FAX 410-560-6107.** Items stocked by these shops are noted at the end of each listing and are coded as follows:

(a) Golden Age Comics
(b) Silver Age Comics
(c) New Comics, Magazines
(d) Pulps
(e) Paperbacks
(f) Big Little Books

(g) Magazines
(h) Books (old)
(i) Movie Posters
(j) Original Art
(k) Toys
(l) Records/CDs,Videos,DVD

(m) Trading Cards
(n) Underground Comics
(o) Premiums (Rings,
 Decoders, etc.)
(p) Comic Related Posters
(q) Comic Supplies

(r) Role Playing Games
(s) Star Trek Items
(t) Doctor Who Items
(u) Japanimation/Manga
(v) Collectible Card Games

ALABAMA

Sincere Comics
4667 Airport Blvd.
Mobile, AL 36608
PH: (251) 342-2603
E-Mail:
sincerecmx@aol.com
(a-c,e,m,p-s,u)

ARIZONA

All About Books & Comics
5060 N. Central
Phoenix, AZ 85012
PH: (602) 277-0757
Web:
www.allaboutcomics.com
(a-g,i-n,p-s,u,v)

All About Books & Comics III
4022 E. Greenway
Phoenix, AZ 85032
PH: (602) 494-1976
Web:
www.allaboutcomics.com
(c,g,k,l,m,p-s,u,v)

All About Books & Comics V
810 S. Ash
Tempe, AZ 85281
PH: (480) 858-9447
Web:
www.allaboutcomics.com
(c,g,k,m,p-s,u,v)

CALIFORNIA

Terry's Comics
Buying all 10¢ & 12¢
original priced comics
P.O. Box 746
Atwood, CA 92811-0746
PH: (714) 288-8993
Hotline: (800) 938-0325
FAX: (714) 288-8993
E-Mail:
info@terryscomics.com
Web: www.terryscomics.com
(a,b,d-h,m,n,q)

Collectors Ink
2593 Highway 32
Chico, CA 95973
PH: (530) 345-0958
E-Mail:
bev@collectorsink.com
Web:
www.collectorsink.com
(a-c,e,g,k-n,p-v)

Mile High Comics
12591 Harbor Blvd.
Garden Grove, CA 92840
PH: (714) 741-2096
E-Mail:
gardengrove
@milehighcomics.com
Web:
www.milehighcomics.com

Geoffrey's Comics
15900 Crenshaw Blvd.; Ste. B
Gardena, CA 90249
PH: (888) 538-3198 (toll free)
FAX: (310) 538-1114
E-Mail:
info@geoffreyscomics.com
Web:
www.geoffreyscomics.com
(a-c,g,i,k,m,n,p,q,s,u,v)

Golden Apple Comics
7711 Melrose Ave.
Los Angeles, CA 90046
PH: (323) 658-6047
Web: www.
goldenapplecomics.com
(a-c,g,i-q,s-v)

Lee's Comics
1020-F N. Rengstorff Ave.
Mountain View, CA 94043
PH: (650) 965-1800
E-Mail:
Lee@LCOMICS.com
Web: www.LCOMICS.com
(a-g,j-v)

Golden Apple Comics
8962 Reseda Blvd.
Northridge, CA 91324
PH: (818) 993-7804
Web: www.
goldenapplecomics.com
(a-c,e,g,k-n,p,q,u,v)

Pacific Comic Exchange, Inc.
P. O. Box 2629
Palos Verdes Peninsula,
CA 90274
PH: (310) 544-4936
FAX: (310) 544-4900
E-Mail: sales@pcei.com
Web: www.pcei.com
(a,b,g,i,j)

A-1 Comics
5800 Madison Ave.
Sacramento, CA 95841
PH: (916) 331-9203
(a-m,p-s,u,v)

San Diego Comics
6937 El Cajon Blvd.
San Diego, CA 92115
PH: (619) 698-1177
E-Mail:
rockofeasy@ad.com
Web: www.
sandiegocomics.com
(a,b,c,g,h,n)

Lee's Comics
2222 S. El Camino Real
San Mateo, CA 94403
PH: (650) 571-1489
E-Mail:
Lee@LCOMICS.com
Web: www.LCOMICS.com
(a-g,j-v)

COLORADO

All C's Collectibles
1113 So. Abilene St. #104
Aurora, CO 80012
PH: (303) 751-6882
(a-d,g,k,m-p,s,u,v)

Mile High Comics
Market Square
Shopping Center
1155 South Havana Unit 45
Aurora, CO 80012
PH: (303) 695-9664
Web:
www.milehighcomics.com

Mile High Comics
760 S. Colorado Blvd.
Denver, CO 80246
PH: (303) 691-2212
Web:
www.milehighcomics.com

Mile High Comics
98 Wadsworth Blvd.
Lakewood, CO 80226
PH: (303) 238-8125
Web:
www.milehighcomics.com

RTS Unlimited Inc.
P. O. Box 150412
Lakewood, CO 80215-0412
PH: (303) 403-1840
FAX: (303) 403-1837
E-Mail: rtsunlimited@earth-link.net
(a,b,c,q)

Mile High Comics
60 W. Littleton Blvd. #105
Littleton, CO 80120
PH: (303) 730-8160
Web:
www.milehighcomics.com

Mile High Comics
9201 N. Washiington
Thornton, CO 80229
PH: (303) 457-2612
E-Mail: thornton
@milehighcomics.com
Web:
www.milehighcomics.com

DELAWARE

Captain Blue Hen Comics
280 E. Main St. #101
Newark, DE 19711
PH: (302) 737-3434
FAX: (302) 737-6201
E-Mail: cbhcomic@dca.net
Web: www.
captainbluehen.com
(a-c,g,k-n,p,q,u,v)

GEORGIA

Comic Company
1058 Mistletoe Rd.
Decatur, GA 30033
PH: (404) 248-9846
FAX: (404) 325-2334
E-Mail: mail
@comiccompany.com
Web: www.
comiccompany.com
(a-c,g,k,m,p-r,u,v)

Heroes Ink
2500 Cobb Pkwy. NW
Suite A-3
Kennesaw, GA 30152
PH: (770) 428-3033
(a-c,e,g,k,m,p,q,s,u,v)

Odin's Cosmic Bookshelf
Killian Hill Crossing
360 Killian Hill Rd.,
Suite G-5
Lilburn, GA 30047
PH: (770) 923-0123
FAX: (770) 925-8200
E-Mail: odins@aol.com
(a-c,e-g,j,k,m-r,u,v)

ILLINOIS

Graham Crackers Comics Ltd.
120 N. Bolingbrook Dr.
(Rt. 53)
Bolingbrook, IL 60440
PH: (630) 739-6810
(c,g,k,l,m,q,u,v)

Graham Crackers Comics Ltd.
69 E. Madison
Chicago, IL 60603
PH: (312) 629-1810
(b,c,g,k,l,m,q,r,s,t,u,v)

Graham Crackers Comics Ltd.
2652 North Clark St.
(Lincoln Park)
Chicago, IL 60614
PH: (773) 665-2010
(c,g,k,l,m,q,r,u,v)

Graham Crackers Comics Ltd.
901C Lucinda Ave.
Dekalb, IL 60115
PH: (815) 748-3883
(c,g,k,l,m,q,u,v)

The Paper Escape
205 West First St.
Dixon, IL 61021
PH: (815) 284-7567
(c,e,g,k,m,p-s,v)

Graham Crackers Comics Ltd.
5223 S. Main St.
Downers Grove, IL 60515
PH: (630) 852-1810
(c,g,k,l,m,q,r,u,v)

Graham Crackers Comics Ltd.
2047 Bloomingdale Rd.
Glendale Heights, IL
60108
PH: (680) 894-8810
(c,g,k,l,m,q,r,s,t,u,v)

Graham Crackers Comics Ltd.
1271 Rickert Dr. 135
Naperville, IL 60540
PH: (630) 355-4310
(a-d,g,i-n,p,q,u,v)

Graham Crackers Comics Ltd.
610 S. Randall Rd.
(at Rt 38)
St. Charles, IL 60174
PH: (630) 584-0610
(c,g,k,l,m,p,q,u,v)

Graham Crackers Comics Ltd.
1207 Butterfield Rd. (Rt. 56)
Wheaton, IL 60187
PH: (630) 668-1350
(c,g,k,l,m,q,s,t,u,v)

INDIANA

Comic Cave
3221 17th Street
Columbus, IN 47201
PH: (812) 372-8430
E-Mail: comiccave
@iquest.net
(b,c,g,k-m,p-s,u,v)

Books, Comics & Things
2212 Maplecrest Rd.
Fort Wayne, IN 46815
PH: (219) 446-0025
FAX: (219) 446-0030
E-Mail:
bct@bctcomics.com
Web: www.bctcomics.com
(a-c,k,p-s,v)

Comic Carnival
9729 East Washington St.
Indianapolis, IN 46229
PH: (317) 898-5010
(a-v)

Comic Carnival
6265 N. Carrollton Ave.
Indianapolis, IN 46220
PH: (317) 253-8882
(a-v)

Comic Carnival
3837 N. High School Rd.
Indianapolis, IN 46254
PH: (317) 293-4386
(a-v)

Comic Carnival
7311 U.S. 31 South
Indianapolis, IN 46227
PH: (317) 889-8899
(a-v)

Downtown Comics
137 E. Ohio St.
Indianapolis, IN 46204
PH: (317) 237-0397
E-Mail: dtc@indy.net
Web: www.dtcomics.com
(a-u)

Downtown Comics - Carmel
13682 N. Meridian St.
Indianapolis, IN 46032
PH: (317) 845-9991
(a-u)

Downtown Comics - Castleton
5767 E. 86th St.
Indianapolis, IN 46258
PH: (317) 885-6395
(a-u)

Downtown Comics - Greenwood
8925 S. Meridian St.
Indianapolis, IN 46227
PH: (317) 885-6395
(a-u)

Downtown Comics - West
8336 W. 10th St.
Indianapolis, IN 46234
PH: (317) 271-7610
(a-u)

Galactic Greg's
1407 E. Lincolnway
Valparaiso, IN 46383
PH: (219) 464-0119
(b,c,k,p-r,u,v)

KENTUCKY

Comic Book World
7130 Turfway Rd.
Florence, KY 41042
PH: (859) 371-9562
FAX: (859) 371-6925
E-Mail: cbwinfo@one.net
Web: www.
comicbookworld.com
(a-d,g,k,m,n,o,q,r,u,v)

Comic Book World
6905 Shepherdsville Rd.
Louisville, KY 40219
PH: (502) 964-5500
E-Mail: cbwdoug@
bellsouth.net
Web: www.
comicbookworld.com
(a-c,g,k,m,n,o,q,r,u,v)

MARYLAND

Geppi's Comic World
1116 N. Rolling Road
Baltimore, MD 21228
PH: (410) 788-0900
FAX: (410) 455-9806
E-Mail: gdoug@
diamondcomics.com

Alternate Worlds
72 Cranbrook Road
Cockeysville, MD 21030
PH: (410) 666-3290
(b,c,g,k-n,p-v)

Cards, Comics & Collectibles
100-A Chartley Drive
Reisterstown, MD 21136
PH: (410) 526-7410
FAX: (410) 526-4006
E-Mail:
cardscomicscollectibles
@yahoo.com
(a-c,f,g,j,k,m,n,p,q,s,u,v)

MASSACHUSETTS

New England Comics
131 Harvard Avenue
Allston, MA 02134
PH: (617) 783-1848
Web: www.
newenglandcomics.com
(a-c,e,g,k-n,p-v)

New England Comics
744 Crescent St.
East Crossing Plaza
Brockton, MA 02402
PH: (508) 559-5068
Web: www.
newenglandcomics.com
(a-c,e,g,k-n,p-v)

76

New England Comics
316 Harvard St.
Coolidge Corner
Brookline, MA 02446
PH: (617) 566-0115
Web: www.
newenglandcomics.com
(a-c,e,g,k-n,p-v)

New England Comics
14A Eliot Street
Harvard Square
Cambridge, MA 02138
PH: (617) 354-5352
Web: www.
newenglandcomics.com
(a-c,e,g,k-n,p-v)

New England Comics
95 Pleasant St.
Malden Center
Malden, MA 02148
PH: (781) 322-2404
Web: www.
newenglandcomics.com
(a-c,e,g,k-n,p-v)

New England Comics
732 Washington Street
Norwood Center
Norwood, MA 02062
PH: (781) 769-4552
Web: www.
newenglandcomics.com
(a-c,e,g,k-n,p-v)

New England Comics
1511 Hancock St.
Quincy Center
Quincy, MA 02169
PH: (617) 770-1848
Web: www.
newenglandcomics.com
(a-c,e,g,k-n,p-v)

New England Comics
FFAST New Comic Service
(Mail Order Only)
P.O. Box 690346
Quincy, MA 02269
PH: (617) 774-1745
Web: www.ffast.com
(a-c,e,g,k-n,p-v)

MINNESOTA
Nostalgia Zone
3149 1/2 Hennepin Ave. S
Minneapolis, MN
55408-2620
PH: (612) 822-2806
Web: www.nostalgiazone.com
(a,b,d-g,m,n,u)

NEBRASKA
**Robert Beerbohm
Comic Art**
P.O. Box 507
Fremont, NE 68026
PH: (402) 727-4071
FAX: (402) 727-4071
E-Mail:
beerbohm@teknetwork.com
(a,b,d-k,n-q)

NEVADA
Silver Cactus Comics I
480 N. Nellis Blvd. #C1A
Las Vegas, NV 89110
PH: (702) 438-4408
FAX: (702) 438-5208
(a-c,e,g,k,l,m,p-s,u,v)

Silver Cactus Comics II
4410 N. Rancho Dr.
Las Vegas, NV 89130
PH: (702) 396-8840
Web: www.
silvercactuscomics.com
(a-c,e,g,k,l,m,p-s,v)

NEW HAMPSHIRE
Rare Books & Comics
James F. Payette
P.O. Box 750
Bethlehem, NH 03574
PH: (603) 869-2097
(a,b,d-h)

NEW JERSEY
JHV Associates
(By Appointment Only)
P. O. Box 317
Woodbury Heights, NJ
08097
PH: (856) 845-4010
FAX: (856) 845-3977
E-Mail:
JHVassoc@hotmail.com
(a,b,d)

NEW YORK
Silver Age Comics
22-55 31 St.
Astoria, NY 11105
PH: (718) 721-9691
PH: (800) 278-9691
FAX: (718) 728-9691
E-Mail: gus
@silveragecomics.com
Web: www.
silveragecomics.com
(a-c,f,g,k,m,n,p-s,u)

Jim Hanley's Universe
4 West 33rd St.
New York, NY 10001
PH: (212) 268-7088
E-Mail:
bob@jhuniverse.com
Web: www.jhuniverse.com
(a-c,e,g,k-n,p-v)

Amazing Comics
12 Gillette Ave.
Sayville, NY 11782
PH: (631) 567-8069
Web: www.amazingco.com
(a-c,e,g,j,k,m,q,v)

Jim Hanley's Universe
325 New Dorp
Staten Island, NY 10306
PH: (718) 351-6299
E-Mail:
bob@jhuniverse.com
Web: www.jhuniverse.com
(a-c,e,g,k-n,p-v)

NORTH CAROLINA
**Heroes Aren't Hard to
Find**
1957 E. 7th Street
Charlotte, NC 28204
PH: (704) 375-7462
E-Mail: shelton@heroeson-
line.com
Web:
www.heroesonline.com
(a-c,f,g,j,k,m,p,q,r,u,v)

OHIO
Comic Book World
4016 Harrison Avenue
Cincinnati, OH 45211
PH: (513) 661-6300
E-Mail: cbwinfo@one.net
Web: www.
comicbookworld.com
(a-c,k,m,n,p-v)

Bookery Fantasy
16 W. Main St.
Fairborn, OH 45324
PH: (937) 879-1408
FAX: (937) 879-9327
E-Mail:
bookeryfan@aol.com
Web: www.
bookeryfantasy.com
(a-n,p-v)

OKLAHOMA
Want List Comics
(Appointment Only)
Box 701932
Tulsa, OK 74170-1932
PH: (918) 299-0440
We hate SPAM so please call
for our private e-mail address.
(a,b,f,h-k,m)

PENNSYLVANIA
New Dimension Comics
Clearview Mall #250
101 Clearview Circle
Butler, PA 16001
PH: (724) 282-5283
(a-d,f,g,k-n,q-s,u,v)

New Dimension Comics
20550 Route 19,
Piazza Plaza
Cranberry, PA 16066-7520
PH: (724) 776-0433
E-Mail: ndc@sgi.net
Web: www.ndcomics.com
(a-d,f,g,k-n,q-s,u,v)

New Dimension Comics
508 Lawrence Ave.
Ellwood City, PA 16117
PH: (724) 758-2324
E-Mail: ec@ndcomics.com
(a-d,f,g,k-n,q-s,u,v)

Eide's Entertainment
1111 Penn Ave.
Pittsburgh, PA 15222
PH: (412) 261-0900
FAX: (412) 261-3102
E-Mail: eides@eides.com
Web: www.eides.com
(a-q,s-v)

Dave's American Comics
Buying all 10¢ & 12¢
original priced comics
P.O. Box 8198
Radnor, PA 19087-8198
PH: (610) 275-8817
Hotline: (800) 938-0325
FAX: (714) 288-8993
E-Mail:
Dave@terryscomics.com
Web:
www.terryscomics.com
(a,b,d-h,m,n,q)

SOUTH CAROLINA
Planet Comics
2704 N. Main St.
Anderson, SC
29621-4141
PH: (864) 261-3578
E-Mail: service
@planetcomics.net
Web:
www.planetcomics.net
(a-c,e,g,k-v)

Heroes and Dragons
1563-B Broad River Rd.
Columbia, SC 29210
PH: (803) 731-4376
(a-c,k,m,p,r,u,v)

TENNESSEE
The Great Escape
111-B North Gallatin Rd., N.
Madison, TN 37115
PH: (615) 865-8052
(a-c,e-n,p-v)

The Great Escape
1925 Broadway
Nashville, TN 37203
PH: (615) 327-0646
(a-c,e-n,p-v)

TEXAS
**Lone Star Comics
Books & Games**
504 East Abram St.
Arlington, TX 76010
PH: (817) Metro 265-0491
(a-c,e,g,k,m,p-v)

Lone Star Comics
Books & Games
511 East Abram St.
Arlington, TX 76010
PH: (817) 860-7827
FAX: (817) 860-2769
E-Mail: lonestar@
lonestarcomics.com
Web:
www.mycomicshop.com/
(a-c,e,g,k,m,p-v)

Lone Star Comics
5720 Forest Bend Dr.,
Suite 101
Arlington, TX 76017
PH: (817) 563-2550
(b,c,e,g,k,m,p-v)

Lone Star Comics
Books & Games
11661 Preston Rd. #151
Dallas, TX 75230
PH: (214) 373-0934
(b,c,e,g,k,m,p-v)

Remember When
2431 Valwood Pkwy.
Dallas, TX 75234
PH: (972) 243-3439
Web: www.
rememberwhenshop.com
(a-d,g,i,j,m,n,p,q,s,t)

Lone Star Comics
Books & Games
6312 Hulen Bend Blvd.
Ft. Worth, TX 76132
PH: (817) 346-7773
(b,c,e,g,k,m,p-v)

Bedrock City Comic
Company
6717 Westheimer
Houston, TX 77057
PH: (713) 780-0675
FAX: (713) 780-2366
E-Mail: bedrock@flash.net
Web: www.bedrockcity.com
(a-d,f,g,i,j,k,m-q,s-v)

Bedrock City Comic
Company
2204-B FM1960 West
Houston, TX 77090
PH: (281) 444-9763
FAX: (281) 444-9308
E-Mail:
bedrock2@flash.net
Web: www.bedrockcity.com
(a-c,g,j,k,m,n,p,q,s-v)

Lone Star Comics
Books & Games
931 Melbourne
Hurst, TX 76053
PH: (817) 595-4375
(b,c,e,g,k,m,p-v)

Lone Star Comics
Books & Games
2550 N. Beltine Rd.
Irving, TX 75062
PH: (972) 659-0317
(b,c,e,g,k,m,p-v)

Lone Star Comics
Books & Games
3600 Gus Thomasson,
Suite 107
Mesquite, TX 75150
PH: (972) 681-2040
(b,c,e,g,k,m,p-v)

Lone Star Comics
Books & Games
3100 Independence Pkwy.,
Suite 219
Plano, TX 75075
PH: (972) 985-1593
(b,c,e,g,k,m,pv)

Trilogy Shop #2
700 E. Little Creek Rd.
Norfolk, VA 23518
PH: (757) 587-2540
FAX: (757) 587-5637
E-Mail: trilogy2
@trilogycomics.com
Web: www.
trilogycomics.com
(c,l,m,q,r,s,u,v)

Trilogy Shop #1
5773 Princess Anne Rd.
Virginia Beach, VA 23462
PH: (757) 490-2205
FAX: (757) 671-7721
E-Mail: trilogy1
@trilogycomics.com
Web: www.
trilogycomics.com
(a-i,k,m,p-s,u,v)

Another Dimension
130-10th Street N.W.
Calgary, Alberta T2N 1V3
PH: (403) 283-7078
E-Mail: another@
cadvision.com
Web: www.
another-dimension.com
(a-c,e,g,k,n,p,q,s,u)

Introduction:
The Quest for Perfection, Part I

We are graded all our lives. From the moment we are aware enough to understand the importance of what others think about us, we are labored with grades that evaluate our performance, chide us for our flaws, and inspire us to improve. When we are young, we are graded by teachers and professors who scrutinize every aspect of our academic performance and our daily behavior. When we mature and move into the career-minded adult world, we find the same situation awaits us there as well, with supervisors and administrators replacing the teachers. And still we are graded, evaluated, and labeled accordingly at every turn.

In modern American society, we are indoctrinated in this process of relentless, codified evaluation, so it should come as no surprise that even in our leisure-time pursuits - when the pressure of grades would seem to be the thing we would most like to escape - we somehow find a reason to impose those grades on the objects of our desire as well. We are programmed to grade; we simply cannot help ourselves.

Of course, those of us who call ourselves "collectors" have far deeper emotions and impulses driving us than an involuntary impulse to grade. In the case of comic books, for example, we are likely to be driven to find the best example of a given comic as we are to locate any copy at all. Our desire for perfection - or at least its nearest approximation - goes hand in hand with the unceasing force that motivates us to keep collecting these fragile artifacts of the past. This desire is another ingrained behavior, but one that stretches far back into the mists of time, when ancient civilizations held up lofty ideals of beauty and achievement to inspire entire cultures. We collect comic books for their historical and entertainment value, for their artistic and literary merits, for their connection to pleasant memories of a childhood spent with escapist fantasy - but we also collect comics as an exercise in locating and obtaining the best possible examples of the art form. In the realm of collecting - excepting those very few who collect with no regard whatsoever for the physical state of the comics they seek - condition is all, and that is what this book is all about.

That quest for perfection is not without its obstacles, some of which are discussed throughout the rest of this book. A collector may be desperate to find a comic book that resembles its "original" condition as closely as possible, but adversaries from the inanimate - environmental conditions, poor printing materials and machinery - to the living - inconsiderate owners who handled the comic haphazardly - are there to make the search difficult on every level.

Consider, for example, the journey of a typical comic book from the printing press to the newsstand back in the "old days." A publisher would probably print a comic using the cheapest, most volatile materials he could find, triggering the deterioration process at the very moment of manufacture. Next, the printing press and bindery may assemble this stack of pulpy newsprint pages in as lackadaisical a manner as possible, resulting in miscuts, off-center stapling, and even tearing before the comic ever reaches a reader's hands. To prepare them for shipping, these poor comics will now be bound with cord or bundling wire, damaging them further until the top and bottom copies of every stack are deformed to a significant degree.

Then it's off to the distributor, where these ticking time-bomb stacks of comics are tossed with abandon into boxes and onto pallets for delivery to various stores and newsstands. The retailers themselves complete the task by stocking the comics on shelves or loading them into the infamous wire racks, thus assuring that no hopeful comic book enthusiast will ever find a Mint copy of their favorite comic at the local newsstand. Granted, many aspects of the process we have just described have changed drastically since the early days of comics - and markedly improved to be sure - but there can be no doubt that as a fragile physical object subjected to many stages of handling in the journey from the printer to the panelologist, comics frequently begin their life as collectibles with quite a few strikes against them.

But there are other, more devastating opponents railing against collectors than the many machines and individuals who make up the chain of manufacturing and distributing comics - and they are the collectors' younger selves and peers! As Walt Kelly said in 1971 (through his comic strip creation, Pogo), "We have met the enemy and he is us." Kelly was referring to humanity's degradation of the environment through apathetic littering, and the observation can be just as easily applied to the actions of young comic book readers who - unaware of the emotional and financial value they would one day attach to their precious comics - would treat these future collectibles with all the disdain that quickly-read, rapidly decomposing paper pamphlets deserve. Running roughshod over their comic books, tearing covers, patching holes with tape, applying name tags, cutting coupons, rolling them into tight tubes and stuffing them without a second thought into pants pockets, stuffing them into bureau drawers - all this and more might have been perpetrated on a comic by the very same people who would one day spend months or even years desperately seeking a high grade copy of the same issue. In the quest for perfection, the most frequent and pernicious enemy is the collector's own past.

Then again, we have to admit that we do owe these children - our younger incarnations - a debt of gratitude. If it weren't for the punishing treatment they afforded so many comic books of the past, then high grade copies would be far more plentiful even with the volatile nature of the paper and other ingredients. The hobby would be much different today if so many of these comics were easy to find in decent shape, and corresponding valuations would be considerably lower. So perhaps when a collector gripes that the copy of **Batman #100** he so wants to buy has a rolled spine or a missing back cover, he might stop to think that there might be no hobby at all without defects!

The Overstreet Comic Book Grading Guide, First Edition, came about in 1992 when the need for an all-in-one volume covering this highly subjective aspect of comic book collecting became acute. That book also introduced the 100 Point Grading Scale and the Overstreet Whiteness Level, or OWL, for evaluating paper quality in comics. While it proved to be very popular with the comics community and remains a sought-after publication, a lot has changed in ten years. The 100 Point Scale became 10, third-party certified grading entered the industry, and the Overstreet grading standards continued to evolve to reflect the changing needs of a fluid marketplace. The time is now right for a new **Grading Guide**, and we hope this book accomplishes the formidable task of illustrating the many factors involved in grading comic books at least as well as the first edition.

Given the vast scope of a subject like grading comics - a topic that generates at least as many fervently held opinions as there are comics on Earth to grade - we cannot expect to be as comprehensive as we would like, nor do we presume to claim that this book represents the only possible approach to the task of grading and evaluating comics. From this point on, everything contained in these pages should serve as a guide to grading and nothing more. We hope that this book clarifies some of the ambiguities, enlightens you about aspects of grading you may not have known before, and further enhances your enjoyment and appreciation for the hobby of comic book collecting.

Bob Overstreet & Arnold T. Blumberg
September, 2002

The Evolution of Grading

The grading of comic books has never been a static enterprise. As the years have gone by and the hobby has matured, both the methods and standards of grading comic books have undergone a gradual but undeniable evolution. While some of the most dramatic changes in grading have taken place in the last several years alone, there has always been a slow but steady development in existing standards and the ways in which comic book enthusiasts look at the many factors involved in grading comics.

After all these years, the current comic book grading scale and the related nomenclature still bears the mark of its progenitors in two other major collectible disciplines - coins and stamps. In fact, even though stamps shared some similarity with comics when it comes to determining condition - i.e. they are both composed of paper - it was the grading system used by coin collectors, many of whom took up comic book collecting as well, that was adapted for use by our hobby. As a result, comic book grading still labors under the weight of coin-based terminology that, while not wholly appropriate when applied to comics, has nevertheless long since passed into common usage and will not be debated further in these pages.

While the grading standards for comics grew out of a similar system for coins, both have undergone changes as their respective hobbies have evolved. Additions and adjustments to the existing scales speak to a need for ever more detailed evaluation of the collectibles in question. Some might wonder why we clamor for such intense scrutiny, but then one need look no further than the educational system to see where our understanding of and later appreciation for detailed evaluation was first born.

When one attends some traditional nursery schools, only two grades are required to describe student performance:

S	Satisfactory
U	Unsatisfactory

As the child progresses to kindergarten, this system expands:

+	Above Average
	Average
-	Below Average

By elementary school, a far more familiar 5 point system has taken shape:

A	Excellent
B	Above Average
C	Average
D	Below Average
F	Failing

Eventually, even that scale expands to fit the needs of older children and adults, resulting in the full and all too familiar grading system that almost all of us know very well:

A+	Superb
A	Excellent
A-	Excellent Minus
B+	Above Average Plus
B	Above Average
B-	Above Average Minus
C+	Average Plus
C	Average
C-	Average Minus
D+	Below Average Plus
D	Below Average
D-	Below Average Minus
F	Failing

Of course, letter grades and the related nomenclature are only part of the story. Most of us are also very familiar with the numerical 100 point system for evaluating academic work.

Employed as is or in a percentage format, the 100 point numerical grading system can be matched to the letter scale, but with a far greater range of accuracy and detail than what is possible with the letter scale alone. Just as our experience with an evolving system of educational evaluation has introduced us to nomenclature and a 100 point grading scale, so too did the coin and comic book hobbies employ similar systems as their need for more advanced grading criteria intensified.

In the 1932 edition of **The Star Rare Coin Encyclopedia**, compiled and published by the Numismatic Company of Texas and B. Max Mehl - the foremost numismatics authority of his time - a system for grading coins was detailed that parallels the standards adopted by the fledgling comic book hobby about twenty years later. At the time of the **Encyclopedia**, the scale for grading coins was fairly simple:

Proof
Uncirculated or As Minted
Fine
Good
Fair
Poor

This 6 point system evolved, with two new grades inserted into the scale to enable coin collectors to grade with a higher degree of accuracy and detail:

Proof
Uncirculated
Extra Fine or Extremely Fine
Very Fine
Fine
Good
Fair
Poor

Later, the coin hobby settled on a 70 point scale still in use by coin collectors and coin grading services. But for the relatively newborn comic book collecting hobby, the original coin grading scale - with the Proof grade dropped - served as a somewhat ill-fitting but convenient way to begin the process of developing a comic book grading system. By the mid- to late 1950s, the 5 point scale adopted from the coin world was in common use for comics:

Mint
Fine
Good
Fair
Poor

Interestingly, many comic book dealers balked at adopting any kind of grading system, rigidly adhering to a bizarre "no grading" policy. Mail order ads of the time would often include statements like "Please do not make inquiries about condition" or "Inquiries about condition will not be answered." Comic book collectors today would no doubt cringe to see such declarations and give those dealers a wide berth; indeed, it was pressure from collectors of the day who demanded grading information prior to purchase that forced the issue and resulted in the adoption of the first comic book grading scale. Ads then frequently featured statements like "All comics guaranteed to be in good or better condition" or the gloriously vague "All books are in Good to Mint condition unless otherwise noted."

At any rate, the 5 point system soon gained two middle grades, creating a 7 point scale:

Mint
Very Fine
Fine
Very Good
Good
Fair
Poor

It was at this point that mail order dealers, discovering that the mere use of the word Mint resulted in better sales, decided to create new grades that enabled them to keep the word Mint in play even when the comic in question didn't warrant the grade. As phrases like "Nearly Mint" proliferated in advertising, a new middle grade shortened to Near Mint made its debut and became common by the early 1960s. The comic book grading scale now settled into its most familiar 8 point incarnation:

Mint
Near Mint
Very Fine
Fine
Very Good
Good
Fair
Poor

It's also worth noting that for a while, the Very Fine and Very Good grades were not considered "full grades" on par with the others on the scale, but were instead known as "half grades" that rested halfway between the adjacent grades. The adoption of Near Mint therefore caused a bit of a stir - resting between Mint and the "half grade" of Very Fine, Near Mint was a difficult grade to pin down. Was Very Fine now 1/3 of the way to Mint while Near Mint was 2/3, or was Very Fine still a "half grade," with Near Mint 3/4 of the way to Mint? While the matter was eventually settled in the 1989 **Overstreet Comic Book Price Guide**, these three middle or "in between" grades soon gained "full grade" status and today occupy an equal place on the scale with the other grades.

With the release of the first **Overstreet Comic Book Grading Guide** in 1992, a new 100 point scale was applied to the existing grading nomenclature in the interests of even greater accuracy and a heightened level of descriptive detail:

98-100	Mint
90-97	Near Mint
75-89	Very Fine
55-74	Fine
35-54	Very Good
15-34	Good

5-14	Fair
1-4	Poor

This became known as the ONE - the Overstreet Numerical Equivalent - and in concert with the new paper quality grading scale, dubbed the Overstreet Whiteness Level, or OWL, a new era in comic book grading began.

By the end of the '90s, however, it was clear that further refinement was needed. The 100 point system, while more accurate - perhaps - and descriptive, was a bit too complex, often leading to confusion as to exactly where within a particular sub-range a specific comic fell. In attempting to enhance the descriptive potential of the comic book grading scale, the 100 point system had introduced an intense level of detail that jarred some users of the scale.

In addition, even newer middle grades had come into use throughout the hobby over the years. Most were employed by dealers and collectors on a colloquial basis to try to express condition with more specificity than the current system could not provide, while others came into being when unscrupulous types tried to convince buyers that a comic in a particular condition was actually in better shape by using the terminology of the next higher grade in concert with the real grade. By the end of the '90s, the hobby was replete with "middle grades," "plus/minus grades," and "split grades." Clearly, order had to be made of chaos.

By 1999, through the participation of many of the hobby's most prominent dealers, collectors, and enthusiasts, a new 10 point version of the scale was created that essentially moved the decimal place in the 100 point system while introducing a few minor tweaks as to the placement of certain grades along the scale. The new system also incorporated the most widely used "plus/minus" and "split" grades, rigorously anchoring them to the scale and establishing their positions with regards to the other grades. The result was the 10 point scale that debuted in the 30th edition of the **Overstreet Comic Book Grading Guide** in 2000.

Apart from a minor modification to the nomenclature for 10.0, which now becomes Gem Mint (GM) as of this new edition of the **Grading Guide**, the system remains the same as it did when it first appeared in the 2000 **Overstreet Comic Book Price Guide**. Note, however, that calling it the "10 point" system is a bit misleading - while it does indeed use a numerical scale from 0 to 10, the scale actually features 25 distinct grades and their numerical equivalents.

The comic book grading scale has certainly evolved over the last fifty years, and there's no reason why we shouldn't expect that evolution to continue as the hobby itself grows and develops with time. For now, however, this **Grading Guide** will provide you with as much information as possible concerning the current scale and its usage. We hope that this book will enhance your understanding of comic book grading and enable you to utilize the 10 point system to evaluate your own comic books with a greater degree of accuracy and satisfaction.

10 Point Grading Scale

10.0	GM	Gem Mint
9.9	MT	Mint
9.8	NM/MT	Near Mint/Mint
9.6	NM+	Near Mint+
9.4	NM	Near Mint
9.2	NM-	Near Mint-
9.0	VF/NM	Very Fine/Near Mint
8.5	VF+	Very Fine+
8.0	VF	Very Fine
7.5	VF-	Very Fine-
7.0	FN/VF	Fine/Very Fine
6.5	FN+	Fine+
6.0	FN	Fine
5.5	FN-	Fine-
5.0	VG/FN	Very Good/Fine
4.5	VG+	Very Good+
4.0	VG	Very Good
3.5	VG-	Very Good-
3.0	GD/VG	Good/Very Good
2.5	GD+	Good+
2.0	GD	Good
1.8	GD-	Good-
1.5	FR/GD	Fair/Good
1.0	FR	Fair
0.5	PR	Poor

The Quest for Perfection, Part II: Preservation and Storage

Often, one of the most powerful elements of the collector's impulse is the desire not only to own a cherished comic book but to find the best possible copy as well - there's not as much satisfaction in locating a threadbare **Amazing Fantasy #15** that looks like it lined a birdcage for twenty years than there is in discovering a brilliant white, high-gloss copy with no hint of acidic odor. Even collectors who find what they're looking for will frequently "upgrade" to a better copy when the opportunity arises. The quest for perfection in collecting is never-ending.

Unfortunately, it's also a potentially futile enterprise, particularly when you consider the kind of collectibles that comic book enthusiasts are seeking. There are a number of powerful adversaries awaiting collectors, not least of which are the comic books themselves, or rather the effects of time on their components. After all, these comics were not manufactured for the long haul. They were built to last but a short time - utilizing acidic newsprint paper, thin covers, inconsistent inks, occasionally damaging bindery machinery - and bound not for a Mylar snug or a CGC slab but for a child's back pocket and eventually the nearest rubbish bin. Comics were intended as disposable fare, but collectors now apply the most stringent archival regulations on a class of collectible that was ephemeral at best.

Is there any way to combat the ravages of time on this collection of degrading organic materials and circumvent the inexorable force of entropy, which dictates that all things eventually break down? Well, we might not be able to keep comics in Gem Mint condition forever, but we can slow the process with tried and true methods of preservation and storage.

Some of the best advice for preserving a comic is simply to handle it carefully. Most dealers and collectors hesitate to let anyone personally handle their rare comics, and it is common courtesy to ask permission before handling another person's comic book. Most dealers would prefer to remove the comic from its bag and show it to the customer themselves. In this way, if the book is damaged, it would be the dealer's responsibility and not the customer's.

When handling high grade comics, always wash your hands first, eliminating harmful oils from the skin before coming into contact with the books. Lay the comic on a flat surface or in the palm of your hand and slowly turn the pages. This will minimize the stress to the staples and spine. In basic handling situations:

Step 1: Remove the comic from its protective sleeve or bag very carefully (more detail can be found in "How to Grade")

Step 2: Gently lay the comic unopened in the palm of your hand so that it will stay relatively flat and secure.

Step 3: Leaf through the book by carefully rolling or flipping the pages with the thumb and forefinger of your other hand. Be sure the book always remains relatively flat or slightly rolled. Avoid creating stress points on the covers with your fingers and be particularly cautious in bending covers back too far.

Step 4: After examining the book, carefully insert it back into the bag or protective sleeve. Watch corners and edges for folds or tears as you replace the book. Always keep tape completely away while inserting a comic in a bag.

While it may seem a bit excessive, careful handling of an exceptional book can go a long way to preserving its condition for some time to come. But that's only the beginning. Careful storage is also a key element in the preservation of a cherished book. Since comic books are composed of such volatile materials, they must be protected from the elements, as well as the dangers of light, heat, and humidity. This can be accomplished with certain storage methods, but remember: improper storage methods will be detrimental to the "health" of your collection, and may even quicken its deterioration.

Store comic books away from direct light sources, especially florescent light, which contains high levels of ultraviolet (UV) radiation. UV lights are like sunlight, and will quickly fade the cover inks. Tungsten filament lighting is safer than florescent lighting, but should still be used at brief intervals. Remember, exposure to light accumulates damage, so store your collection in a cool, dark place away from windows.

Room temperature must also be carefully regulated. Fungus and mold thrives in higher temperatures, so the lower the temperature, the longer the life of your collection. Like UV, high relative humidity (rh) can also be damaging to paper. Maintaining a low and stable relative humidity, around 50%, is crucial. Varying humidity will only damage your collection.

Atmospheric pollution is another problem associated with long term storage of paper. Sulfuric dioxide, which can occur from automobile exhaust, will cause paper to turn yellow over a period of time. For this reason, it is best not to store your valuable comics close to a garage. Some of the best preserved comic books known were protected from exposure to the air, such as the Gaines EC collection. These books were carefully wrapped in paper at the time of publication and completely sealed from the air. Each package was then sealed in a box and stored in a closet in New York. After over 40 years of storage, when the packages were opened,

you could instantly catch the odor of fresh newsprint; the paper was snow white and supple, and the cover inks were as brilliant as the day they were printed. This illustrates how important it is to protect your comics from the atmosphere.

Now that we understand a bit more about the environmental impact on comic book condition, what of the actual storage materials themselves? Care must also be taken when choosing materials for storing your comics. Many common items such as plastic bags, boards, and boxes may not be as safe as they seem; some contain chemicals that will actually help to destroy your collection rather than save it. Always purchase materials designed for long-term storage, such as Mylar sleeves and acid-free backing boards and boxes. Polypropylene and polyethylene bags, while safe for temporary storage, should be changed every three to five years.

Comics are best stored vertically in boxes to preserve flatness and spine tightness. If you choose to store your comics on shelves, make sure that the books do not come into direct contact with the shelving surface. Use acid-free boards as a buffer between the shelves and the comics. Also, never store comics directly on the floor; elevate them 6-10 inches to allow for flooding. Similarly, never store your collection directly against a wall, particularly an outside wall. Condensation and poor air circulation will encourage mold and fungus growth.

Ultimately, nothing will prevent the deterioration of a comic book collection, but as examples like the Gaines collection have proven, there are occasions when even unintentionally well-stored comics can avoid the aging process for a considerable length of time. With some care in handling and attention to the materials used for comic book storage, your collection can enjoy a long life and maintain a reasonable condition for years to come.

Shipping Your Comics

by Dale Moore

Getting the highest price for your prized comic book is of paramount importance to collectors and investors alike. It is the popular consensus that mindful archival storage aids in the preservation of a comic book collection and maintains grade assignment as well. Additionally, careful handling and shipping of books also play roles in assuring that the transition from buyer to seller does not negatively affect grades.

Whether acting through catalogs, the Internet, or simply sending your books to a third-party grading service such as CGC, the sender must realize that careful packaging, obeying courier regulations, and properly insuring the books are conducive to maintaining the book's current grade.

Careful Packaging

To properly package comics for shipping, you will need backing boards, Mylar or regular comic book bags, cardboard (cut a little larger than bag size), a suitable size box, and additional materials like scotch tape, packing peanuts, bubble wrap, and large envelopes.

Place the comic and backing board into a Mylar sleeve or regular comic bag. Do not use cardboard inside the comic bag, and do not put more than one comic in a single bag. Avoid using tape to seal Mylar sleeves. Remember: "Tape is not your friend!" (Thank you, Scott Talmadge). Any involvement with comic books suggests that only scotch tape - or "magic" tape - should be used. Duct, shipping, and even masking tape will be destructive if it accidentally comics into contact with comic books. Save these kinds of tape for the outside of your packages only.

You should place no more than five books in between two pieces of cardboard and then slide them into a large envelope to prevent book migration. You may use scotch tape to secure the cardboard if no envelope is available. It is not recommended that you tape the books directly to the cardboard.

Now you are ready to surround the books with bubble wrap, paper shredding, or other packing protection to provide "bumper padding" for all sides of the comics. Place the books into the box, making sure they are not too loose. You should be able to send upwards of thirty books using this simple method. For larger shipments, consider using comic boxes, one covering the other, and taped together securely.

When sending books to a customer, don't forget to include an invoice or a receipt. When sending books to a third-party grading service, be sure to include an invoice and a method of payment.

To sum up: pack securely, include payment or receipt, and address accordingly.

Obey Courier Regulations

Consult your courier service representative for comprehensive details. The methods recommended here are based on USPS (United States Postal Service) guidelines.

- Fill out customs forms if shipping outside the US; avoid "gift" and "sample" categories.
- Make sure your claim value is equal to your insured value.
- Do not use priority envelopes or boxes as packing materials for the inside of your package unless you are recycling.

*Dale Moore is a former writer, collector, and dealer of comic books; consultant to **The Official Overstreet Comic Book Price Guide**; former advisor to **Comic Book Marketplace** and Ixtlan Entertainment; President and CEO of the non-profit Comics4kids effort; and Quality Control specialist at Comics Guaranty, LLC.*

- Do not invert boxes to avoid paying priority shipping.
- Keep in mind that if you must make an insurance claim, your item will be opened and your claim may suffer if you have already defrauded your courier.
- Do not rule out the use of media mail, as most ads in comic books have expired, and they may not be excluded from the media mail classification.

Insurance

It is always in the best interest of all parties to insure your books. Come to terms with a figure that you are comfortable with. For instance: how much would it actually cost you to replace the books at current market price? Or perhaps you are content with having only your original purchase price reimbursed.

You can assess the replacement value by consulting local dealers, **The Official Overstreet Comic Book Price Guide**, and searching completed eBay auctions. If you have no access to these sources, you might consider taking your cost price and multiplying it by three to determine your replacement value.

The more attention you pay to careful packaging, obeying courier regulations, and insuring your books, the more likely it is that you will preserve the delicate grade of your books and obtain satisfactory results in the secondary marketplace.

How to Grade a Comic Book

While it takes time to hone grading skills and become a true expert, there is a general step-by-step process that anyone can follow to evaluate a comic and arrive at a reasonable estimation of the book's grade.

Step 1: Lay the comic down on a flat, clean surface. If it is in a plastic bag or a Mylar sleeve, carefully remove it, being sure not to snag the comic on any exposed tape or adhesive fastener on the bag flap. In some cases, it might be wiser to remove the tape entirely first, or fold it down until it adheres to the bag itself and cannot catch the cover of the comic when it slides out.

Step 2: Make sure your grading area is well-lit, moisture-free and smokeless. Do not let direct sunlight fall on the comic, and do not put the comic under any unfiltered fluorescent light which may generate ultraviolet (UV) rays - the same bleaching agent emanated by sunlight. Normal incandescent lighting is best.

Step 3: Review the general exterior look of the comic and find a comparable example in the Grading Guide pictorial sections. Double-check your selection by comparing the comic to pictorial examples in the nearest adjacent grades as well.

Step 4: Carefully examine the exterior of the comic from front cover to back cover, identifying all defects, such as: condition of staples; creases, folds, and tears; soiling, staining and discoloration; ink brightness and cover gloss; and the other defects detailed throughout the Grading Guide.

Step 5: If any defect warrants reducing the grade from your original selection, compare the comic with the next lowest grade to see if it more accurately represents the condition of the comic you are grading. Note that even the smallest flaw on the cover can be a determining factor - after all, the cover is the first thing anyone will see, and its condition is the principle concern of collectors to determine the book's grade and over all "eye appeal."

Step 6: Carefully examine the spine of the comic. Next to the cover, this is the most important area for evaluating the comic's grade.

Check for rusted staples, stress lines, tears, spine roll, and other such defects.

Step 7: Examine the inside front and back covers and check for further defects like tearing, creasing, and yellowing. Pay particular attention to the area where the interior of the comic meets the covers. NOTE: Do not open the cover of higher grade books to more than a 45 degree angle to avoid stressing the spine.

Step 8: Confirm that the centerfold and all pages are still present and check their condition.

Step 9: Estimate the whiteness level of the interior pages. You might wish to use the Overstreet Whiteness Level (OWL) card to assist you in determining the general hue of the paper. Please note, however, that the OWL card - while still available and used by many comic book enthusiasts - is no longer strictly up to date with the current grading standards and 10 point system utilized in this second edition of the Grading Guide.

Step 10: Locate and identify interior defects such as chipping, flaking, possible brittleness, and other flaws. In all cases, keep comparing the comic to the examples depicted in the pictorial grade section you selected to either confirm your choice or further refine your selection.

Although this is a generalized method of grading that should serve most collectors well enough, the expertise and experience required to reliably grade comic books accurately is not easy to come by. For as much as some have tried to make comic book grading a science, it remains more of an art form, and even the most seasoned graders still make the occasional error. While novices should not expect to become superb graders overnight, they may be able to avoid the common pitfalls by following the standards set down in this Guide. A few other suggestions:

• Get a second opinion from a veteran grader or another collector as a "reality check."

• NEVER grade a large quantity of comics at one time. You will almost certainly "burn out" - your concentration will flag and you will miss crucial details when evaluating later comics that may seriously affect your determination of grade.

• Try to keep samples of actual comic books in various grades for ready comparison.

• The middle of the 10 point scale remains the murkiest area of comic book grading. Pay special attention to all the little factors that push a comic from Very Fine/Near Mint down to Very Fine, or from Very Good up to Fine. Even the most experienced graders in the world can sometimes slip up on those transitions.

• When purchasing a comic, always ask to see the interior before you buy it. This protects both parties in the transaction. You can ask the seller to show you the interior rather than presume to handle the comic yourself, and this ensures that you will incur no liability should handling of the book result in further damage. This will also enable the seller to prove to you that he or she is hiding no additional defects in the interior of the comic that might detract from the over all grade. After all, a book with superb eye appeal on the outside cover may still harbor a secret or two within. Ask anyone who collected mid-'70s Marvel comics, and they'll tell you about all the Marvel Value Stamps that are missing from those letters pages. Above all, when dealing with comic book sellers, be polite and honest as you would expect them to be.

Grading is inherently a subjective enterprise, and no matter how specific the criteria, differences of opinion can arise. Collectors on either side of the equation should respect the right of the other party to their opinion as to a comic's grade, if that opinion can be reasonably supported by the physical evidence. Discussion can sometimes result in a compromise. Ultimately, a buyer can always just walk away from a transaction if they are unsatisfied with the book or the grade.

How to Describe a Comic Book

In the old days, mail order was the life's blood of the comic book collecting world, and while a great deal of mail order business still goes on, many readers of this book will doubtless be buying and selling comics on Internet auction sites like eBay. No matter what the venue, the principles of honesty and full disclosure still apply. Above all, you want to convey to any potential buyers all pertinent details about the comic for sale and its condition. In the case of eBay listings, for example, while you have as much space as you need to provide an exhaustive description on the item page itself, you have a limited amount of space to convey important details in the title description that will appear in any general item search. Succinct use of terminology is key in making sure that everyone knows what you mean when you offer a comic book for sale.

Below we present some guidelines for describing a comic book in a single line of text. These are merely suggestions, but remember that it's probably best to provide too much information rather than too little; informed buyers are happy buyers.

Relevant information about a comic book can be listed in the following order:

TITLE - **Detective Comics**, **Amazing Spider-Man**, **Night Nurse**, etc.

ISSUE NUMBER - #5, #121, #0, V3#4, etc.

GRADE OR GRADE ABBREVIATION - VF/NM, GD+, FR, etc.

ADDITIONAL INFORMATION ON CONDITION - Short notes on interior defects, restoration specifics if necessary, etc.

SUPPLEMENTARY INFORMATION ON COMIC - Is it a pedigree, does it feature a first appearance, does it have a classic cover, etc.

PRICE - $14.95, $92, $1,500, $42 ea., etc.

Traditionally, comics were usually listed for sale as follows. Note that the exact style of describing the grade has not always remained consistent:

Amazing Spider-Man V2#36 near mint

All-Star #3 vg+ (small chip out lower left, minor color touch URFC, first JSA)

Fantastic Four #1 fair (severe water damage, small piece out LLFC, research copy)

Amazing Mystery Funnies V2#7 Very Fine+ (Mile High copy, unrestored, intro Fantom of the Fair, Near Mint except for 1/2" tear LRBC, white pages)

With the advent of a simplified numerical scale, more collectors than ever before have taken to describing a comic book grade by its number rather than its nomenclature. For example, someone might now say "I have a 9.0 **Incredible Hulk** #181" rather than "I have a Very Fine/Near Mint copy of **Incredible Hulk** #181." Whether you believe the numerical grade equivalent is enough or whether you favor the nomenclature, it is best to use both when describing a comic book for sale. Today, the four comics listed above might be described as follows:

Amazing Spider-Man V2#36 NM 9.4

All-Star #3 Very Good+ 4.5 (small chip out lower left, minor color touch URFC, first JSA)

Fantastic Four #1 Fair 1.0 (severe water damage, small piece out LLFC, research copy)

Amazing Mystery Funnies V2#7 VF+ 8.5 (Mile High copy, unrestored, intro Fantom of the Fair, NM except for 1/2" tear LRBC, white pages)

The Quest for Perfection, Part III: Comic Book Restoration

Restoration - the word carries with it a lot of baggage, particularly in today's comic book market. Once considered an acceptable and at times even desirable way to preserve and/or revive aging key comics to some semblance of their original glory, restoration has today become a source of considerable debate in the hobby.

When restoration of comics first began, it was a collection of crude, damaging attempts to preserve or fix comics exhibiting defects like tears or missing pieces. At first, collectors employed unsophisticated methods, using tape, glue and color pens to repair their books. Restoration soon evolved, however, and skilled professionals (and plenty of aspiring amateurs) began to utilize more advanced techniques like chemical baths and deacidification to not only repair comics but restore them to a more desirable condition.

Today, professional restorers work in a constantly evolving field using methods that have stood the test of time. Unfortunately, the value of comic book restoration itself has undergone a major re-evaluation in recent years, leading to a general downturn in the opinion of most collectors as to the desirability of a restored comic.

The stigma that has attached itself to the restoration of comic books has less to do with the actual results of professional, reliable restoration methods than it does with the poor results of amateur restoration, and more alarmingly, the unethical behavior of many amateur restorers and dealers who have concealed such repairs from buyers and passed off restored books as original condition collectibles. Such behavior has severely affected the overall opinion of restoration in the comic book marketplace. In the quest for perfection, restoration now occupies a shadowy corner that has not yet been fully illuminated.

Without honest and full disclosure of restoration on a given book, and without a greater understanding of the many methods involved in preserving and/or restoring comics, restoration is likely to continue to suffer a negative reputation in the comic book market. In this section, we hope to clarify some aspects of this aspect of comic book collecting, as well as present one possible way to evaluate such restoration.

Although the term 'restoration' applies to a wide range of preservative and restorative methods, it could be argued that there are three distinctly different types of processes at work in the catch-all category of restoration:

Preservation: This type of restoration applies to comics where no materials have been substantially added to the original comic. Work has been done to preserve the comic's own paper and structure, with minor repairs to prevent further damage and deterioration. Preservation can include securing a loose staple, small tear or sealing a minor hole by refastening the folded paper flap back to the page. Traditionally, attempts to preserve a comic as well as possible without actually 'restoring' it to any degree have been known as 'conservation.' Whatever the term, it implies a decision to leave the book in its current state while preventing further decay.

Restoration: This is the middle ground, containing comics that have had minor preservative and restorative work done in order to prevent or slow further damage and decay and revive the original appearance of the existing materials. Restoration can include minor tear and hole repairs, minor color touch or removal of soil to reveal original color, and possibly staple replacement.

Reconstruction: This area includes comics that have had extensive repair work or have had significant amounts of new material added to the existing comic. Comics that have had large portions of a cover corner, chunk or interior page reconstructed and recolored or illustrated, comics that have been assembled from the pieces of several other lower grade examples, and comics that have had extensive repair work that significantly transformed the condition of the original comic can be considered reconstructions. Some might even say these comics are now not truly a legitimate representation of an actual original copy of that book but rather a newly created collectible out of the ashes of the old, but that is a debate for another time.

Currently, Comics Guaranty LLC (CGC) employs a series of abbreviations to designate states of Extensive, Moderate, and Slight restoration as follows:

EA	Extensive Amateur
EP	Extensive Professional
MA	Moderate Amateur
MP	Moderate Professional
SA	Slight Amateur
SP	Slight Professional

(See Matt Nelson's essay for more on these levels of restoration.)

CGC also uses a purple label to distinguish restored certified books from unrestored books, which are usually encapsulated with a blue label. The purple label itself has gained a certain level of notoriety due to the industry-wide stigma carried by the notion of restoration. For many, receiving a purple label from the grading company is a fate worse than death, but this attitude may yet change with time.

On the following pages, we present two viewpoints on restoration. First, we offer an essay by Susan Cicconi-Killiany of The Restoration Lab. Susan contributed to the first edition of the **Grading Guide** ten years ago, and she returns here to once more provide some much-needed background on the processes of restoration, from telltale signs of restorative work to recommendations on when to restore and when not to restore a comic book. Finally, she takes a brief look at the impact of CGC and what lies ahead.

Next, Matt Nelson of Classic Conservations proposes a new way to evaluate comic book restoration using separate numerical scales for assigning values to various aspects of restoration along qualitative and quantitative lines. Matt's suggested scales and definitions, and the ideas presented by both contributors, do not represent the end of the debate by any means - in fact, this may be the start of a whole new chapter in the history of comic book restoration. It is our hope, however, that by presenting these suggestions in this forum, we can further stimulate the ongoing discussion about this often hotly contested area of the hobby.

The Restoration of Comic Books: 1982-2002

by Susan Cicconi-Killiany

When I started restoring comic books in the early 1980s, the question most frequently asked of me was, "Can you make my book look mint?" Twenty years later, isn't it funny that the question remains the same...but for very different reasons. Several factors have contributed to these changes over the years, and I would like to address some of them in this article.

The Definition of the Word "Restoration"

The word restoration, as defined by the Webster dictionary, means to "repair," to "renew," or "give back." Using archival materials and conservationally sound techniques, my role as comic book restorer is to "repair" these books to what was once their original condition. Complete restoration entails taking the book apart; cleaning the cover; pressing out the interior pages; solvent washing to remove tape and tape stains; water washing to remove wrinkles, old glues and discolorations; mending tears and filling in holes; and finally color touching those areas to "restore" the structure and appearance of a timeless collectible. These are all methods that alter the book in a way calculated to improve its condition and to enable it to last longer than it would have in its original, unrestored condition.

The vast majority of comic books were printed on highly acidic newsprint - the cheapest grade of paper available - and, for the most part, were not intended to be permanently preserved. Who could have imagined that comic books bought at the newsstand for 10 cents would eventually command such incredible prices - depending on condition and rarity - some fifty years later? The need for professional conservation is the inevitable result of increased cultural appreciation for "old comic books," as well as high prices. Most comic books submitted for restoration are generally soiled and torn with often well-intentioned - but regrettably naive - attempts at repair using various mending glues and adhesive tapes. In most cases, the extent to which some books have been treated has rendered these attempted repairs irreversible. Since my role as paper conservator is, in part, educational, the following checklist may help collectors identify these unskilled attempts at restoration. With a little practice, collectors can learn to readily recognize these.

1. COLOR TOUCH-UP (COLOR TOUCH)

(a) Ball point pen - Shiny when viewed at a raking light, blue and black; (b) Felt-tip pen - Bleed through to inside of cover, especially reds, blues, greens, purples, and black; (c) Water color - Bleed through when incorrectly applied; opaque and pasty when incorrectly applied.

Most likely areas for color touch-up: (a) Exterior of front and back covers; (b) Exterior of spine at stress marks, hairline creases, and along black lines; (c) Corner creases and folds. **Note:** When examining for Color Touch-Up, it is

After studying paper conservation in Paris and restoring 36 original drawings by Pablo Picasso, Susan Cicconi-Killiany returned to Boston to apprentice in the field of comic book conservation under the tutelage of William Sarill. In 1986, she took over The Restoration Lab and for 16 years has built a tremendous reputation in this field. In the '90s, she was Sotheby's restorer of choice for their historical collectible auctions. Her latest work in decoupage art has landed her a major gallery on Cape Cod, which is a testament to her fine skills and expertise. Please visit her site at www.spiritofflowers.com and enjoy yet another masterpiece.

*Exterior of **Detective Comics #29** before restoration (left) and after (right).*

necessary to gently look along the inside of the spine for bleed-through. Special care should be exercised during the examination as improper handling may result in damage to the comic book. **Warning:** NEVER use ball point pen or felt tip pen for color touch for any reason.

2. MENDING PAPERS

(a) Look for mending at areas of support, including staple holes, along spine, and at edge tears. Open the cover to expose the inside of the spine at staple holes; (b) Check both sides of centerfold at staple holes for any mended tears as these tears can be very small.

Note: When examining for mending papers, it is necessary to gently look along the inside of the spine for bleed-through. Special care should be exercised during the examination as improper handling may result in damage to the comic book.

3. MISSING PIECE REPLACEMENT

The most likely areas for Missing Piece Replacement are along spine, corners, and margins ("Marvel Chipping"). Carefully hold comic book up to the light, open front and back covers - one at a time - so that each half can be viewed in front of the light.

4. COVER RE-GLOSSING

If cover looks excessively glossy and is heavier and thicker to the touch, chances are it has been sprayed with a fixative which will result in irreversible damage.

5. MECHANICAL OR "DRY" CLEANING

Difficult to detect unless there are noticeable streaks and spots where erasures have been incorrectly used.

Note: DO NOT CONFUSE this with traditional laundry dry cleaning which uses the solvent Carbon Tetrachloride. This solvent is extremely toxic and flammable and should never be used in a poorly ventilated area and/or near open flame. Never use this solvent on paper for any reason.

6. CHEMICAL OR "SOLVENT" CLEANING

When correctly performed, impossible to detect. When incorrectly performed, covers will retain the transfer stain and/or a possible residual chemical odor.

7. AQUEOUS OR "WATER" CLEANING

If incorrectly treated, covers and interior pages will feel flimsy, light, and will warp and cockle. There is also the possibility of color fading.

8. TAPE REMOVAL

Look for residual yellow or brown stains that are rectangular in shape. Locations will vary throughout cover and interior, with more emphasis on support areas (spine, corners, centerfold).

9. STAPLE REPLACEMENT

This is a difficult detection. Staples should be viewed from the inside, that is at the centerfold page. Look to see that the points of the staple which meet are tight and pronounced. Prongs of staple should line up perfectly to any indentations in the paper. It is almost impossible to replace original staples in their precise location.

10. SPINE ROLL REMOVAL

When correctly done it is impossible to detect. When incorrectly performed, you'll still see the spine roll.

11. DEACIDIFICATION

This process requires professional expertise. Improper application can result in irreversible damage. Covers which have been incorrectly sprayed can result in color flaking, ink bleeding, and "cockling." Interiors may warp and/or severely darken.

12. BLEACHING

When incorrectly treated, covers and interiors will be excessively white and gritty with washed out or faded colors. A residual foreign odor is sometimes present.

13. TRIMMING

Probably the most difficult to detect. This is most visible on Silver Age books - DC, Marvel, EC. Most of these books have a very slight overhang or "over-cover" (1/16") at the top and bottom margin of front and back covers. Because of improper storage or handling, the cover will crease at the top and eventually tiny tears will form. Attempts have been made to alter the book, irreversibly, by trimming the excess margin flush with the interior pages. Trimming is often suspected if the interior pages are flush on the top and bottom of the margin, unless it is a book of extremely high grade with no other evidence of repair. Interior pages have also been found to be trimmed. Snags in the paper are visible and the trimmed edges are usually slightly lighter in color than the rest of the book.

Professional Comic Book Conservation

The conservation of comic books fulfills two

*Interior of **Detective Comics #29** before restoration (left) and after (right).*

95

primary functions: restoration and preservation. Professional restoration methods may include a variety of techniques, such as general non-abrasive cleaning, tape and stain removal, paper reinforcement/replacement, and color inpainting. Professional restoration is a very meticulous process which emphasizes structural as well as aesthetic enhancement. The materials used must be of the highest quality. The craftsmanship must always strive to maintain the highest standard of excellence and professionalism.

The key word is professional. Only professional restoration can increase the value of comic books. Take, as an example, a 1940 VG copy of a **Batman** #1. It is worn and torn with a spine that is frayed and splitting; the cover is slightly soiled and discolored with creases and stress marks; it has a severe spine roll. This comic appears almost "lifeless." Upon closer examination, the cover has no pieces missing, colors are still vivid and not faded. There is no evidence of previous restoration, tapes, or other adhesives. The interior pages are supple and tanning and the staples are clean and tight. This copy of **Batman** #1 is an optimal candidate for restoration. Through a series of very careful and

meticulous procedures - cleaning, paper reinforcement, spine repair, color inpainting, pressing, and possibly deacidification - this **Batman** #1 will now have a Very Fine appearance and is preserved for many years to come. The comic book is structurally sound and tight, pages will remain supple, colors are cleaner and therefore brighter - in short, this **Batman** #1 lives once again!

These basic but often painstaking techniques of restoration can be applied to most Golden Age books. It has been my experience that early **Detective**, **Batman**, **Action** and **Superman** (all DC publications) are prime candidates for restoration because of paper malleability and responsiveness. There are exceptions, however, since particular compositions of inks, fiber furnish, and fiber sizes varied from one publisher to another. **Marvel Mystery** and **Captain America** (Timely publications), for example, will react differently to certain procedures - not necessarily adversely - but the paper stock of these comics is not as cooperative.

The most difficult books to restore are the Silver Age titles such as **Amazing Spider-Man**, **Incredible Hulk**, **Fantastic Four**, **X-Men**, **Avengers**, etc. (all Marvel publications). The

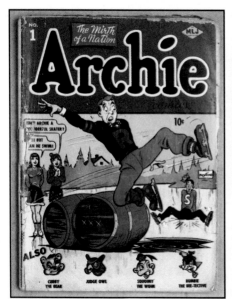 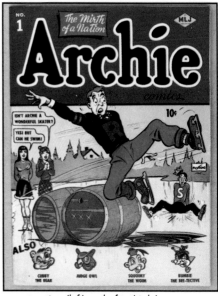

*Exterior of **Archie Comics #1** before restoration (left) and after (right).*

Interior of **Archie Comics #1** before restoration...

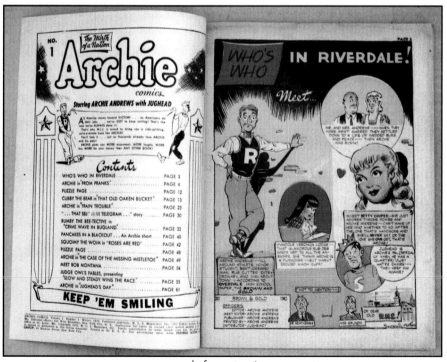

and after restoration.

paper composition of these books differs greatly from Golden Age comics with respect to size, weight, colors and inks. Because of these complex properties, it is necessary to carefully choose between structural and aesthetic repair. Experience has shown that it is best to take care of defects that affect the book structurally, such as tears, loose or rusted staples, spine rolls, creases and folds. A simple solvent wash - as opposed to a water wash - will greatly improve the book visually by removing the "yellowing" particularly present in these early Marvel titles. This is sometimes referred to as a "transfer stain," since ink particles have migrated to the inside covers from the first and last pages. This is not to be confused with "browning," which is an actual acid transference of the interior pages onto the cover, breaking down the cellulose paper fibers and causing them to age and discolor. This yellowing can be completely removed with no adverse effects to dimensions (size), gloss (ink reflectivity), or color. The cover is cleaner, whiter and colors are brighter.

The comics of Disney and EC Publications fall in between Golden Age and Silver Age with regard to restoration potential. Disney is closer to Golden Age with its large format, 16 folios, and heavier stock paper. Structural and aesthetic repair are performed with excellent results. EC Comics resemble those of early Marvel titles where the emphasis is more on structural repair. The covers and interior pages of numerous EC Comics show signs of advanced aging and discoloration (browning). Many of these books will benefit from deacidification; this must be done while the pages are still flexible.

Annuals and other "square-bound" (perfect bound) comics such as **World's Fair** and early **World's Finest** are in a special class by themselves. These books generally contain several pages held tightly with large heavy staples, and the covers - composed of a thick pulpy stock - are glued directly onto the spine of the interior pages with very strong adhesive. It is extremely difficult to treat these covers unless they are loose, frayed and splitting away from the interior. If possible, mechanical separation would be required for

restoration. If the cover is not loose yet needs cleaning, pressing, and possible tear reinforcement - which is very often the case - then the process can only be accomplished within certain limitations.

What are the Right and Wrong Candidates for Complete Restoration?

My basic rule of thumb is that any comic book in Fine or better condition should be left alone and untouched. In my opinion, because of the demand for unrestored books in today's high-grade investment market, these books should be left unrestored. This being said, I still have collectors who insist that it is for their own personal collection. They want their book sound and solid and to look as nice as it possibly can. These people are always thrilled with the outcome and tell me that it is the best money they have ever spent.

I truly feel that any books with tape on them or exhibiting evidence of previous attempts at restoration should definitely be restored. Tape over time will just continue to permanently discolor and ruin the cover or interior pages. If pages are fragile and on the brink of becoming

*A copy of **Showcase #4** before restoration...*

...and after restoration.

There are two general guidelines that can be used to determine if a comic book is a candidate for restoration:

A) Items should be worth at least $1500 in their present condition.

With rates at $100 per hour, it is not cost effective to request a full structural and aesthetic enhancement on an item of lesser value unless unique conditions exist.

B) Always consider structural repair before aesthetic repair.

Tear and spine reinforcement, cleaning or replacing rusted staples, spine roll removal, general cleaning and pressing of creases and folds, and/or solvent wash can all greatly contribute to the structural support of the book while also enhancing its visual impact.

Additionally, if budget permits, missing piece replacement at corners and at the top and bottom of the spine, followed by color inpainting, will ultimately complete and enhance the book's aesthetic impact. There is nothing wrong with color inpainting provided it is applied onto the filled area and not used as a measure to mask stains and discolorations.

All in all, it is important to consider the proper techniques necessary to insure that comic books retain their suppleness, cover lustre, and page whiteness; these are simple measures such as proper storage in a heat-, light- and humidity-controlled environment, the use of archival preservation supplies, and - when necessary - deacidification of interior pages. Restoration, when done professionally, can greatly enhance the longevity of these fragile, valuable, and rare paper treasures.

What is NOT Considered Restoration?

In the second paragraph, I used the word "alter," and I feel that this is a very important distinction. When you alter something, you are by definition changing it. For example, collectors with very high-grade expensive books ask me about cleaning the staples. You can have a beautiful comic book, but unfortunately the staples are rusting and you can see the build-up on the outside, and

brittle, then I strongly advocate deacidification to at least arrest and neutralize the destructive acids found in these paper pulps.

An important point that people don't consider is that restoration is not purely cosmetic; in the long run, it's really about preservation and saving the book. Professional restoration on the right candidate enables the book to maintain and hold its value and not de-value over time.

Having discussed some of the best candidates for restoration, it is also important to recognize when NOT to restore a comic book. On occasion, rare books of high grade are submitted for restoration because the cover is missing a miniscule piece at the margin or there is a slight pencil marking or hairline crease with color loss. Other than these minor defects, the books were beautiful copies, sound and flat, clean with supple pages, tight staples, etc. It is my strong feeling and the consensus of most seasoned collectors that the appropriate course is to leave these books in their natural, unrestored state. Repairing any of these tiny defects is NOT true restoration.

in some cases at the centerfold. In order to clean the staples, you have to remove them from the book. This may not seem like such an intrusive operation, but I truly feel that once you remove staples from a comic book, you are altering the book; therefore I would consider this restoration. It is almost impossible to put the original staples back in the same exact way as when the book was manufactured. Noticing that staples have been removed from a comic book will always open a book up to suspicion as to whether anything else may have been done to the cover or interior pages.

There are very few and specific cases that I would define as non-altering, or non-restoration. These books are usually high grade condition copies with a slight wave to the cover, or a very slight dent or crease, or even a very slight smudge in a white area of the cover; there can also be slight dents in the interior pages. There is absolutely nothing being taken apart, or any kind of addition to the book to change its original unrestored structure or appearance.

The Advent of CGC

I do feel that having a professional grading service is good for the comic book industry. Books need to be evaluated, examined and ultimately documented for the prospective buyer or investor. Comic book investment has shown itself to be a steady and profitable market, and year after year, prices only seem to escalate for high grade items; this is where I come in.

I am not a dealer, a grader or a collector. However, I have been in the restoration business for twenty years, repairing hundreds of key Golden and Silver Age comics. I also provide a restoration detection service where I thoroughly explain in writing where and what kinds of restoration have been performed on a particular book. If the book is unrestored and in its original state, I provide a written statement with my signature stating such. If available, I also like to include the history of the book, its provenance, and how many owners have exchanged this particular copy. I do not put the book in any type of enclosure. This service is available on high grade

comics only. These are all factors I consider in my evaluation of these very select and particularly high grade investment comic books. When you are making an investment worth thousands of dollars, it is always good to have another opinion.

Twenty Years and Still Learning

In 1982, I was still apprenticing with the pioneer of comic book restoration, William Sarill, in downtown Boston. I can't tell you the number of **Action** #1s, **Batman** #1s and **Superman** #1s we were turning over in those days; Silver Age wasn't even around the shop. Some of the things that were attempted on those books, I wouldn't even dream of doing today. Since I took over the reins of The Restoration Lab in 1986, I have always maintained a more conservative approach to comic book restoration. The skills I learned in Paris apprenticing on 20th Century fine art drawings, most notably Pablo Picasso, I still employ today - basic, sound, conservationally accepted techniques that will provide the best care for that particular piece of timeless art.

Ten years ago, the prime candidates for my services wanted complete restoration by any definition. Today the majority of my client base is much more educated about their investment potential and are willing to pursue perfection. Because of my detailed expertise and twenty years of handling all of the key Golden and Silver Age books, what was once a candidate from VG to VF+ for complete restoration has now evolved from VF to NM without any alterations to the books whatsoever. Whether my clients are keeping or selling their books, the feedback is consistently positive and their comic book's value has been increased.

With the incredible investment market for comic books, it's very hard to remember the good old days of enjoying your comic book for what you truly remembered it to be. I will always put forth my very best intentions and efforts to heal a timeless collectible like a **Superman** #1 or an **Amazing Fantasy** #15, and I continue to educate those who are still buying a comic book to restore for nostalgia's sake or to invest for the future.

A Restoration Proposal

by Matt Nelson

Professional restoration became a legitimate enterprise in the 1970s, but was initially ignored as a profit tool and instead used mainly by collectors who wished to make their comics look as perfect as possible. There was no consideration given to candidacy or the effect on value.

Restoration reached a fever pitch in the '80s and early '90s, evidenced by the increasing number of comics being restored and the high prices paid for them, regardless of the extent and quality of the work. The resultant profit made it an extremely lucrative business, but one critical factor was missing: full disclosure was largely ignored, and many buyers were deceived into buying books under false assumption that they were unrestored or only restored to a lesser degree. As a result, restoration developed a tarnished image by the end of the decade.

With the advent of certification in 2000, collectors' trust began to build again, although the bloated prices of the '90s still lingered. The market has seen an adjustment of restored values since then, eliminating the large profit margins enjoyed by sellers in previous years. This is essential to re-establishing a strong market - restoration should not be viewed strictly as a money-making device, but as a way to preserve our treasures for future generations.

Extent of work

Currently, there are three categories used to describe the extent of restoration on a particular comic book. Below are allowable repairs for each:

Slight

- Cover cleaned
- Cover re-glossed (amateur)
- Color touch (very light in nature, a few hits on the spine or edges)
- Minor support or seals using glue (amateur)
- Minor support or seals using rice paper and adhesive (professional)
- Replaced or cleaned staples

Moderate

- Color touch (along spine and edges, used for piece replacement)
- Small piece replacement (bindery chips, Marvel chipping, small and few in nature)
- Numerous support areas or tear seals

Extensive

- Large piece replacement
- Color touch (large areas impainted, whole areas recreated)
- Reconstructed interiors
- Recreated pages or parts of cover

It is possible that a book may only have repairs in the Slight category, and yet receive a Moderate label. This is due to the cumulative amount of work exceeding what is allowable in the slight range.

Quality of work

No two restored comics are alike. Technically speaking, a fully restored comic should be NM, because the book exhibits no tears, missing pieces, spine splits, tape, or loose centerfolds. All defects have been repaired, and yet each restored book can receive a different "apparent" grade. While some restoration jobs do not

Matt Nelson is the owner of Classic Conservations, one of the top restoration services in the nation, and is recognized as a leading expert on the conservation and marketing of restored books, as well as pedigreed comics, encapsulation, and Golden Age material. He has written several features for CBM, including the Unseen Gold series and a definitive compilation of pedigreed collections.

*A copy of **Detective Comics #28** before restoration (left) and after (right).*

repair every single defect on a given book, the true measurement used to determine grade is the quality of work. Color touch is the best indicator of quality, followed by piece replacement and cleaning. What is most important when grading restored comics is the "feel;" the closer a restored comic feels to an unrestored copy, the higher the apparent grade. Acquiring the ability to grade by feel takes time, and requires handling many restored comics.

Restoration Removal

Since certification began, the market has seen an even greater demand for unrestored comics, pushing some to consider removing restoration from their books in order to achieve the coveted "blue label" from CGC. While this may prove to be financially beneficial in the short run, one must consider the long-term effects of removal, including defacement and changing market conditions. Even when removing slight restoration, it is sometimes necessary to scrape, dig, cut, and obliterate parts of the comic itself. This is especially true for removing amateur restoration, such as glue and color touch that

has bled through the paper. The grade of a comic will almost always suffer upon removal of restoration.

Considering how young the certified market is, patience should be exercised when considering a candidate for restoration removal. As the number of certified comics compounds over the coming years, the true rarity of pre-1960 comics in unrestored condition will become obvious, making slightly restored copies more desirable, especially considering their relative value.

The best candidates exhibit professional restoration that can be safely removed with minimal risk to the book itself. This includes tear seals and support using rice paper and water-soluble adhesive, as well as acrylic and water-based color touch. Cleaned covers are irreversible, as are cases of trimming, re-glossing, and replaced staples. Removal should not be attempted on comics with Moderate or Extensive restoration due to the damage that could occur and the resulting significant decrease in grade. By these standards, it is safe to say that 90% of restored comics are not worthy candidates for removal.

PROPOSED SCALE FOR GRADING QUALITY OF RESTORATION
(on a scale of 1-9, 1 being the best)

CLEANING
Water Cleaning
1 Color has original feel. Still looks aged, sizing job is good, paper doesn't feel coarse or chalky. Cleaning is almost invisible.

5 Cleaning is apparent, but not obvious. Cover may be stiff or too glossy. Tint of aging doesn't quite match pages, due to bleaching. Professional work, but not nearly invisible.

9 Cover may be re-glossed, or not sized at all. Paper is bleached; all aging is gone, making the cleaning obvious. Paper feels chalky or coarse and flimsy.

Dry Cleaning
1 Light cleaning to white areas only. Does not affect gloss or colors. Invisible.

5 Some color affected by cleaning, including smudging by erasing arrival dates, writing, etc. White areas may be obvious, especially if the rest of the book is exceptionally dirty.

9 Paper is coarse or worn from rubbing. Loss of gloss and major color smudging from cleaning; very obvious.

Solvent Cleaning
1 Invisible, nothing on the book to give any indication of use, such as chemical smell or staining.

5 Minor signs of use, including smeared ink, ring stains, and/or light tape residue not fully removed.

9 Inks have run, staining, residue, worn spots from rubbing.

Staple Cleaning
1 Cleaned, but near invisible. Only removed staples offer clues.

5 Cleaned, but obvious…i.e. silver staples set against rust stains on the paper underneath.

9 Staples have been replaced, or placed in crooked (amateur work).

Page Cleaning
1 Cleaned and feels natural to the touch. Size is not altered in any way, and pages do not exhibit any puffiness or coarseness. Near invisible.

5 Pages may have a faint smell (chemical or otherwise), or feel slightly coarse (no or very little sizing replaced), puffy, or not aligned properly.

9 Heavily washed, colors have faded somewhat, paper coarse to the touch, puffy from improper pressing, and pages not properly aligned. Cockling or warping has occurred.

STRUCTURAL REPAIR
Glue Repair
1 Minor placement at typical areas of comic, including top and bottom of spine (bindery chips), along spine (feathering), or tear seals. Glue is hard to detect by touch, and is not visible in any way. Non-abrasive glue, including water-soluble glue or removable adhesive.

5 Apparent, but unobtrusive repairs that may exhibit shininess or a rough feel. Visible tears that have been sealed, and interior paper stuck to the cover.

9 Includes sloppy application that is very apparent to the naked eye. Any type of glue can be used, particularly irreversible glue that may have stained the paper or attracted dirt. Amateur work of spines glued together, long tears and re-attached pieces.

Tear Seal
1 Invisible, mainly involving lap tears that need only adhesive to seal. These tears are usually small and do not exhibit any wear or dirt along edge. Rice paper used in very small quantity may also fall into this category if near invisible.

5 Typical tear seals involving rice paper and adhesive. Rice paper is visible, although tear may be cleaned well enough to appear invisible from other side, especially with color touch applied.

9 Very visible seals done with rice paper or any similar product, and may be applied with non-archival adhesive. Tear is dirty and jagged, and adhesive may be shiny or coarse to the touch, with generous application of rice paper applied in amateurish fashion.

Support

1 Usually applied along spine or corners that have weakened. Application involves rice paper that has been used very sparingly, and blends well with comic paper. Near invisible to the eye.

5 Placed along edges of cover (Marvel chipping) or spine. The support is visible, although done in a professional fashion with archival materials.

9 Very visible. Includes sloppy or amateur application using non-safe materials, such as irreversible adhesive or obvious Japan (or other) paper.

Piece Fill

1 Near invisible, using actual comic parts. Fill is seamless and can only be spotted by holding book up to a light. Tint of interior paper matches perfectly, and no support is required.

3 Typically found in most restoration jobs, including fills using rice paper or some other foreign material to comic paper, and requiring color touch. Application is professional, and looks sharp. Hard to spot at first glance—blends well, although seam can be found if examined.

6 Professional work that may not have been performed to the best of ability. Color touch does not blend well, replaced piece is obvious, especially along the seam. Edges of replaced paper is uneven or trimmed crooked.

9 Amateur work that is very apparent to the eye. May use non-archival material such as regular paper, marker color touch, and white glue for adhesive. Professional application could suffer from bad color touch work or visible seam with non-matching tint of interior paper.

Graft

1 A professional replacement of a large area of a cover, using a piece from another cover of the same book. Paper tint must match near per-

*A copy of **Fantastic Four #1** before restoration (left) and after (right).*

fectly, and appear seamless. Near invisible.

5 Professional techniques used, but work is more visible to the eye. Replacement may include parts from another comic, or a sharp repro of another cover ("remanufactured" or Xerox). All missing parts of cover must be filled, including text area on inside. Paper tint is a close match.

9 Amateur application using a crude Xerox or hand-drawn copy of missing piece. May be taped or glued in, and will usually not include text area on inside cover. Colors do not match well, and the different feel of the paper is obvious. Seam is obvious.

AESTHETIC REPAIR
Color Touch

1 Invisible, with use of acrylic or watercolor. Color blending is perfect, and can be picked up only with a blue light. Application is very sparing, applied only to the exact areas in need of color touch. Usually found on spine stresses and creases or color flakes.

3 Not obvious at first or second glance, but visible to the eye when examined closely. Colors blend when viewed in a raking light, and applied sparingly. No bleedthrough or signs that give its location away.

5 Well applied color touch that uses non-archival materials such as markers, pen, colored pencils, crayons, or paint of some kind. Usually light in nature, and blends well.

7 Typical color touch found. Professional in application, but matching is not perfect. Colors may appear off to the eye, especially in areas of half-tones where a flat color was applied. May appear flat in a raking light, or feel different to the touch. Can be heavily applied if blended well, but usually found in moderate amounts on piece replacement.

9 Amateur application, using non-archival material such as markers, pen, colored pencils, crayons, or paint of some kind. Bleedthrough occurs. Watercolors or Acrylic

can be used, but matching job is horrible, and very apparent when examined.

Staple Replacement

1 Invisible, with only examination of prongs at centerfold giving replacement away. Staples match the age of the book. Alignment is perfect, and prongs are bent to appear as originally placed. There is no wear around the staple holes, and no extra holes were made in the paper upon replacement.

5 Staples may align perfectly, but holes have been enlarged by improper insertion, or prongs incorrectly closed. Color of staples may not match age of book. Clean staples are obvious when set against rust-stained paper.

9 Staples are crooked, with large frayed holes created during insertion. Prongs do not lie flat, or have been bent incorrectly. Replaced staples are obvious by being the wrong size, or having an unnaturally new tint.

Page Whitening

1 Pages appear unrestored, with only a slight hint of chemical smell giving them away.

5 Chemical smell is strong; pages appear unnaturally white, but feel natural to the touch.

9 Cockling or warping has occurred from bleaching. Pages feel coarse and puffy. Staples have started to rust from chemical transfer.

Page Replacement

1 Invisible, usually occurring with whole wraps replaced that perfectly match paper tint and size. Staple holes line up.

5 Page tint may be off, or size of page may distinguish it from others. Also, attachment by way of rice paper or adhesive may be apparent, although done in a professional manner.

9 Page(s) glued in at spine, and usually do not match paper tint or line up—appears very obvious. Replacement using incorrect pages or a Xeroxed page as well.

*A copy of **X-Men #1** before restoration...*

PROPOSED SCALE FOR GRADING QUANTITY OF RESTORATION
(on a varying scale of 1-60, 1 being the slighest)

CLEANING

Water Cleaning
1   Yes or No

Dry Cleaning
1   Yes or No

Solvent Cleaning
1   Yes or No

Staple Cleaning
1   Yes or No

Page Cleaning
1   Yes or No

STRUCTURAL REPAIR

Glue Repair
1   Spot of glue at typical locations; top and bottom spine (bindary), feathering along spine and small tears. One or two spots inside spine of cover.

10   Glue along length of spine, rough to the touch. Inside cover may be glued to spine of interior in various spots.

20   Glue in most areas of book (inside or outside of spine) and long tears. Very apparent to the eye (may appear shiny or dirty). Entire spine glued to interior.

Tear Seal
3   Up to one 1" seal, or three 1/2" seals

10   Up to three 1" seals, or six 1/2" seals

20   Up to five 1" seals, ten 1/2" seals, or one 3" seal

40   Up to ten 1" seals or three 3" seals

60   Multiple tear seals, including large tears up to entire length of cover

Support
3   One or two corners supported; partial support to spine area. Or one or two areas along edge no more than 1" in length.

10   Entire length of spine supported, or up to two edges of cover. All four corners up to

1" in size.

20 Entire length of spine, as well as up to all four edges.

Piece Fill

5 One small piece fill, usually bindery chip or corner chip 1/4" x 1/4" in size

10 Two to three small fills, top and bottom spine or corners

20 Four to five small fills or one to two medium fills (dime size)

30 Six to seven small fills or two to three medium fills

40 Eight to ten small fills, four to five medium fills, or 1 large fill (half dollar)

50 Six to eight medium fills or two to three large fills

60 Nine to ten medium fills or four to five large fills or one giant fill (up to 1/4 of cover)

AESTHETIC REPAIR
Color Touch

1 One or two hits on cover

5 Five to ten hits or one concentrated area

(dime size)

10 Eleven to fifteen hits or two to three concentrated areas

20 Twenty to twenty-five hits or five to ten concentrated areas

30 Eleven to fifteen concentrated areas or one large area (3" x 3")

40 Full areas, such as spine, edges or large replaced sections. 20% of cover

50 Full spine, edges. 40% of cover

60 Entire cover painted, 75%-up

Staple Replacement

1 Staples replaced

Page Whitening

20 Pages bleached

Page Replacement

5 Up to one wrap replaced (original)

10 Up to two wraps replaced (original)

20 Up to three wraps replaced (original)

40 Up to four wraps replaced (original)

60 Up to five wraps replaced (original)

...and after restoration.

PROPOSED RESTORATION SCALES: A SAMPLE EVALUATION

QUALITY		QUANTITY	

CLEANING

	QUALITY
Water Cleaning (1-9)	
Dry Cleaning (1-9)	2
Solvent Cleaning (1-9)	1
Staple Cleaning (1-9)	
Page Cleaning (1-9)	
TOTAL	3

CLEANING

	QUANTITY
Water Cleaning (1)	
Dry Cleaning (1)	1
Solvent Cleaning (1)	1
Staple Cleaning (1)	
Page Cleaning (1)	
TOTAL	2

STRUCTURAL

	QUALITY
Glue Repair (1-9)	3
Tear Seal (1-9)	2
Support (1-9)	3
Piece Fill (1-9)	2
Graft (1-9)	
TOTAL	10

STRUCTURAL

	QUANTITY
Glue Repair (1-20)	5
Tear Seal (1-60)	5
Support (1-20)	6
Piece Fill (1-60)	15
TOTAL	31

AESTHETIC

	QUALITY
Color Touch (1-9)	4
Replaced Staple(s) (1-9)	
Page Whitening (1-9)	
Replaced Page(s) (1-9)	
Graft (1-9)	
TOTAL	4

AESTHETIC

	QUANTITY
Color Touch (1-9)	15
Replaced Staple(s) (1-9)	
Page Whitening (1-9)	
Replaced Page(s) (1-9)	
TOTAL	15

QUALITY TOTAL	17

QUANTITY TOTAL	48

DIVIDE BY # OF CATEGORIES USED	7

compare with Extent of Work table below

QUALITY GRADE (round to nearest whole number)	3

EXTENT OF RESTORATION	MOD/EXT

EXTENT OF WORK

Slight	1-5
Slight/Moderate	6-15
Moderate	16-30
Moderate/Extensive	31-50
Extensive	51-up

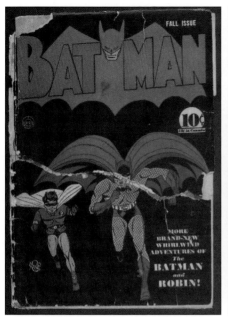

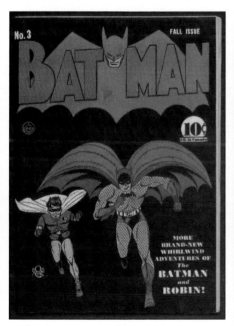

*The demonstration of Matt Nelson's proposed Quality/Quantity Restoration scale at left was based on an evaluation of a copy of **Batman #3**, pictured in its unrestored form (above) and restored (below). This copy has been graded an "apparent" VF 8.0, with moderate/extensive restoration as determined by the scales at left, setting it at a Restoration Rating of 3.*

Grading Victorian and Platinum Age Books

by Tom Gordon

Victorian and Platinum Age comics are the foundation for modern comic books. These early books are historically important as they are the origin of comic books as we know them. They were printed in several formats that are for the most part unlike the modern format of comic books; therefore, they offer a challenge when grading them based on the fact that these books were pro-

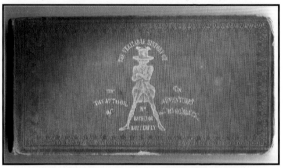

1. History of Mr. Bachelor Butterfly *by D. Bogue (1845).*

duced in a variety of formats, including hardbound, cardboard cover, paper cover, drawing, paint, coloring book format, and others.

The main obvious difference in Victorian and Platinum Age books when compared to later comics is the size and multiple formats used to produce them. Paper quality is also an issue, as the various books were printed with a multitude of different stocks, including tracing paper, cardstock, pulp, book stock paper, and others.

There are several different books from these eras that feature unique formats, such as drawing books and coloring books. These types offer an additional challenge for grading.

1. HARDBOUND FORMAT

This format is found in both Victorian and Platinum Age comics. The Victorian Age examples are typically found in the style of antique books and are hardbound. These types of

comics may have gilted covers or areas. Defects can include loss of gilt and spine damage. This usually occurred when removing the book from the shelf and is unique to this style of book. The Platinum Age examples are usually found in hardbound format, which is made of a heavy stock cardboard instead of the standard fine hardbound book, which is more often seen in Victorian Age editions.

2. CARDBOARD COVER FORMAT

This format of the Platinum Age is usually found in several sizes, including 10x10" and 11x16". Cardboard cover books are also found in numerous sizes. The 10x10" size format was used heavily by Cupples and Leon. In some cases, when a person thinks of Platinum Age comics, they tend to envision this type of comic format. These books feature a cardboard stock cover with a thin cloth binding to the spine. The

---

*Tom Gordon has had a connection to collecting his entire life. He grew up around several generations of collectors and has experienced both the collecting and business side of the hobby firsthand. He is actively involved in comic books and related memorabilia. He has contributed information and photos to numerous collecting guides, including **The Overstreet Comic Book Price Guide**, **Hake's Price Guide To Character Toys**, and others.*

1. Mutt and Jeff Book 3 (1912).

2. Joe Palooka (1933)

3. Barker's 'Komic' Picture Souvenir Part 2 (1900s)

interior pages are stapled together and then glued to the inside of the spine. This format and its larger counterpart have a very common condition defect - they almost immediately receive damage when read. The covers, when opened, tend to cause a separation inside the cover near the spine. This separation occurs when the cover is opened at an angle of more than approximately 45 degrees. This defect is due to the materials and size of the books as well as the lack of flexibility in the materials used. This separation, however, should not be confused with the cover being detached from the interior; in many cases, the cover and interior are still firmly attached. If one were to evaluate a lower grade book, this defect should be factored in as it occurs frequently. If one has a VF or better copy, this defect could lower the grade by perhaps .5 of a grade or so.

3. PAPER COVER FORMAT

This format is in many ways similar to that of modern comic book counterparts. These books are structurally the same as standard paper cover comics. In some cases, they may have a string binding instead of staples, as found in some Victorian Age examples; books with string binding should be graded the

**4. Boys and Girls Big Painting
& Drawing Book** (1914)

same as those with staples. Paper stock used in the manufacturing of these books will greatly affect the conditions in which these books are found. In some cases, the paper is a heavy stock that has little flexibility and actually cannot stand the wear and stress from usage.

4. Buster Brown Drawing Book
CGC 8.0 VF (1904)

4. DRAWING, PAINT, & COLORING BOOK FORMATS

This format is typically found in the Platinum Age. Numerous comics of the era were more than just comics; they were also toys. These books are found in several formats that include both paper covers and cardboard cover formats. As noted in the cardboard format, examples of these books with cardboard covers should be viewed in the same light as those noted above. Typically, Drawing Books and Coloring Books are not found in high grade due to the books having been used as well as read. In some cases, these books may be found used but intact in a fairly acceptable condition. One must take into consideration that they are Drawing Books or Coloring Books when grading them; it would fair to grade these types of books based on the overall condition of the book. If neatly drawn, one could easily have a Buster Brown Drawing Book that structurally grades at VF, but grades FN+ due to the usage of the book.

Due to the numerous formats used in the comic books of the Victorian and Platinum Age, the number of possible variations is enormous. As further examples are discovered, they will need to be included at a later date. These are just some of the examples from the Victorian and Platinum Age and the grading criteria that might be applied to them.

Grading Odd Format Comic Books

by J.C. Vaughn

Bound volume collectors have been grabbing onto important pieces of history for years only to have them denigrated as worthless (or certainly worth less).

Spirit fans have heard for an equally long time from some quarters that **The Spirit** sections aren't comic books.

Origins of Marvel Comics and the other books in the Fireside series have had fans for years, but for many years recognition was hard to come by.

Vampirella, **Planet of the Apes**, **Six Million Dollar Man** and others have long had enthusiastic collectors, but the respect granted to magazines – particularly black and white magazines – within the ranks of comics fandom has been grudging at best in many cases.

Superman vs. The Amazing Spider-Man wasn't only the first meeting of Marvel's and DC's flagship characters, it was an oversized "Treasury Edition" production, another format slow to win acceptance from the general comics collecting audience.

In each successive era, the argument about "What is a comic book?" becomes increasingly difficult to settle. The debate is nothing new, however. Whether with relatively new formats such as hard cover originals and collections or with older presentations such as bound volumes, comic book collectors have been faced with the task of assessing editions that seem to defy normal evaluation.

Much of the problem for collectors may stem from the perceived difficulty of storing items of dissimilar shapes and/or obtaining collecting supplies such as bags, boards or boxes for said items. From the wonders of the Platinum Age to the original Marvel Graphic Novel line to Chris Ware's **Acme Novelty Library** series, though, most of the same things that apply to grading other comics still apply; there are just a few additional considerations to watch out for... keeping in mind that condition is still king.

Bound Volumes

Some collectors want to be able to hold an individual comic book in their hands when they read it - holding a whole volume just doesn't satisfy them the same way. Others, though, have long found such volumes to be a meaningful, quick and relatively easy to collect otherwise hard-to-find items.

In a bound volume, it is frequently possible to get a complete run of a title, often with bright covers and interior pages in Fine or better with the exception of the outer edges, where browning may have occurred.

When evaluating a bound volume, there are several additional areas to assess in addition to the standard grading procedure one would utilize for a single comic book. These factors, not surprisingly, mostly have to do with the binding process used and the actual binding itself. Other areas of concern frequently include paper quality, trimming, tears, notations, the manner in which the bound volume was read, and the frequency with which it was read.

There are varying levels of professionalism evident in binding. This, along with the source of the material, can have significant impact on the desirability of a bound volume.

*J.C. Vaughn is the Executive Editor of Gemstone Publishing. He is a contributor to **The Overstreet Comic Book Price Guide**, **Hake's Price Guide To Character Toys**, the **Scoop** e-mail newsletter, and other publications.*

There are basically two types of bindings for bound volumes - those that are glued together (called "perfect bound") and those that are Smythe sewn (sewed as signatures with no glue). Theoretically, those volumes that are Smythe sewn could be un-bound and restored to single issues by cutting the threads and reinserting the staples into each issue. Most bound volumes are not hand sewn, and there would be glue used on the spines of each book, making it nearly impossible to remove them.

As a result of the binding process, many comics within bound volumes have been trimmed so as to create a uniformed appearance. The edges of those copies that are not trimmed tend to be more ragged (referring to the manner in which they line up staggered or "ragged" when viewed as a stack, not as an indication of damage).

In addition to the appearance of the volume's edges, another reason for trimming was that comics were often made to fit the hardcover material or bindery size that was available rather than finding materials to completely fit or cover the comic book size. The most desirable format would have the hardcover edges protruding very slightly beyond the comics, or at the very least flush with the edges.

Bound Volumes Checklist
- Binding may show varying levels of wear.
- Method of binding may eliminate benefit of removing comics from binding.
- Varying degrees of professionalism in binding may affect desirability.
- Number of comics per bound volume may affect the success of the binding and therefore the desirability of the volume.
- Insect damage is common in bound volumes.
- Paper tears, sometimes depending on the frequency of reading, can be common.

*Two examples of the wildly variant **Acme Novelty Library** series by Chris Ware, which ranges from digest-sized to tabloid-sized issues, along with a DC **Tarzan** treasury edition.*

 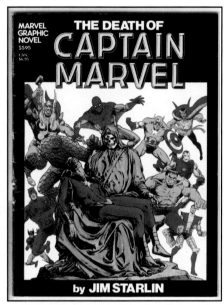

*Two copies of the Marvel Graphic Novel, **The Death of Captain Marvel**, that illustrate the difficulty of preserving black cover editions. Note the extreme spine wear on the copy at right.*

- Finding pages that have been trimmed, sometimes down to – or even into – the art, is common.
- Trimming is frequently uneven between issues.
- Volumes from archives or collections of publishers, creators and others concerned with the production of a particular work may be considered more desirable.
- Volumes from prominent collections may be more desirable.

Spirit Sections

Beginning in June 1940, **The Spirit** sections were sized inserts in many newspapers across the country. Created by Will Eisner, these sections featured the Spirit and other strips, and they carried the local newspaper's imprint. As 16-pagers (later 8-pagers), these sections did not include a separate cover. As such, and without the traditional, more resilient cover stock to protect them, **The Spirit** sections frequently have taken a lot of physical abuse when they show up. Other than their newsprint-based predisposition to more rapidly browning paper, the defects one would typically note on one of these sections are almost the same as one would find on a regular comic book. Additionally, paper condition varies based on which newspaper printed the section. Two Spirit sections of the same date that would otherwise grade the same may be very different based solely on paper quality. The success of DC Comics' line of **The Spirit Archives** has bolstered interest in these sections.

The Spirit sections varied slightly in size, but the standard sections were 7-1/2" or 7-3/4" wide x 10" to 10-1/2" inches high, a bit larger than standard comic books. It's also important to note a very desirable size variant: The **Philadelphia Record/Sunday Bulletin** published an oversize **Spirit** section measuring about 10-1/4" x 15" inches. These are gorgeous and bring premium prices.

A separate problem somewhat unique to these inserts is that some newspapers, notably The Chicago Sun, inserted The Spirit folded but uncut. The edges had a printed notice, "Cut on this line," but these were often cut irregularly and unevenly by careless consumers with scissors, and values on these would be affected accordingly.

This **Betty and Veronica Digest Magazine** is an example of a small-sized comic format that has been popular for decades.

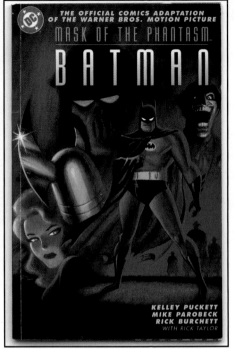

This 5" x 7-11/16" edition of **Batman: Mask of the Phantasm** was packaged with the VHS video cassette. Like many dark colored Prestige Format comics, color cracking is evident along the spine.

Spirit Sections Checklist
- Paper is most often light brown or worse.
- Brittleness is not uncommon.
- Blunted corners are very common.

Magazines

Comics magazines generally lend themselves to the same types of evaluation as comic books. Beyond the obvious (they're just bigger), there are few other items to watch for, mostly based on the notion that the over- whelming number of these publications were sold on the newsstand and not through comic book specialty shops. As such, they're more closely related to Golden Age and Silver Age comics when evaluating them for defects.

An example of the cover roll that can occur on even a recent treasury edition if adverse environmental conditions, like excessive moisture in the air, are present.

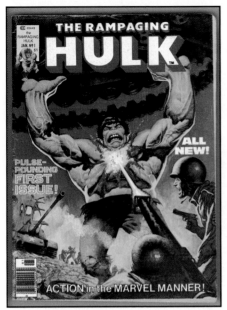

*A copy of the black and white Marvel magazine, **Rampaging Hulk #1**, showing some substantial wear.*

Often these large format comics were displayed standing up like traditional comics. This in and of itself created a set of commonly seen defects, because the Treasury Editions would frequently bend forward, sagging under their own weight. The defects generally associated with this format include spine stress, spine creases, cover creases, and blunted corners.

Alternately, many retailers displayed copies in this format flat, as on the lower magazine racks at a newsstand. This, though, came with its own set of problems. Frequently the cover ink, particularly on darker issues, would rub off on the facing covers when Treasury Editions were stacked (An excellent example of this is **Captain America's Bicentennial Battles**, on which the black ink frequently smudged onto the copy on top or below it).

Magazines Checklist
- Date stamps common on older books.
- Blunted corners common on covers, interior pages.
- Page tears common.
- Staple tears common.
- Rust migration is less likely because of generally superior cover stock.
- Interior page stock is generally heavier, but often cheaper and highly prone to browning.
- Bends, creases or spine stress not uncommon.
- Spine alignment on square bound copies may be in question.

Treasury Editions
With their revival at DC Comics in recent years (mainly featuring the artwork of Alex Ross), the oversized comics generally called "Treasury Editions" (after their Marvel Comics trade name in the 1970s) have made a comeback not only in terms of new product but as collectible back issues as well.

*This 5-15/16" x 8-15/16" **Nowheresville** trade paperback from Image Comics collected (and revised) a mini-series previously published in standard Modern Age comic book format by Caliber.*

Treasury Editions Checklist
- Blunted corners common.
- Page tears common.
- On non-square bound issues, rust migration is less likely because of generally superior cover stock, though it may be present.
- Interior page stock is generally heavier, but often cheaper and highly prone to browning.
- Bends, creases or spine stress common.
- Spine alignment on square bound copies may be in question.

Graphic Novels
Many of the covers on the early **Marvel Graphic Novel** line (and on those from other publishers) featured large areas of black. As a result, many of these editions show white spine cracks ranging in size from almost undetectable to highly visible, book length marks. Various cover defects are the primary detractors for most graphic novels, with the spine being the focal point for most of them. Additionally, where they have been stacked on top of one another, ink smudging problems similar to the Treasury Editions may be found.

Since the graphic novel lines from the major publishers were generally (though not exclusively) printed on a higher-grade paper stock, most issues of paper quality are not a big concern.

Graphic Novels Checklist
- Color cracking on spine common
- Blunted corners common on covers
- On non-square bound issues, rust migration is less likely because of generally superior cover stock, though it may be present

Hardcover Collections & Trade Paperbacks
With the addition to **The Overstreet Comic Book Price Guide** in recent years of the

*Like dust jackets, slip covers should also be graded separately as they too can sustain the same kind of wear visible on book covers and dust jackets. Pictured is a slip cover two-book set of the Fireside editions, **Origins of Marvel Comics** and **Son of Origins of Marvel Comics**.*

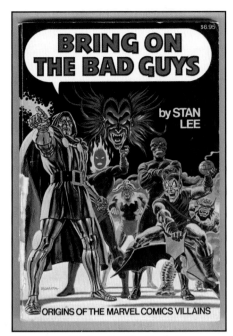

*This copy of **Bring On the Bad Guys**, one of the Fireside series of softcover collections, shows severe spine wear and a complete cover split down the bottom half of the book.*

*Once a popular format of the 1970s, the treasury editions have undergone a revival thanks to projects like DC's **Shazam: Power of Hope** (above), and Image Comics' "Danger-Sized Edition" of **Danger Girl #1** (below).*

Fireside (Simon & Schuster) series, books like **Origins of Marvel Comics** and **Bring on the Bad Guys** have gained in popularity with a wider selection of dealers and collectors.

These books, generally paperback but occasionally hardcover, were among the first of what is now an increasingly sought-after format - the collected edition. (**The Silver Surfer** from 1978 was actually a graphic novel, featuring a new interpretation of the Surfer's origin without the Fantastic Four).

In the contemporary comics market, hardcovers and softcovers play an increasingly important role. DC's Archives series and Marvel's Masterworks collect early, important, or merely popular titles in a format perceived by many to be more impressive to the general public. These books, while a bit pricey, are far more affordable and accessible than the original single issues printed within. Now first printings of these volumes are sought after as collectibles in

The **Marvel Masterworks** hardcovers come with dust jackets; there have been three distinct cover designs so far.

their own right.

When evaluating a hardcover or softcover collection, many of the rules that would come into play evaluating traditional books should be added to those for grading comics. The areas for particular attention include the spine, covers and leading edges of the book. Paper quality is frequently higher than traditional comics, though this is not always the case.

Hardcovers may also feature dust jackets when originally released, which can also suffer damage common to comic book covers and may even be absent on some copies if removed by a previous owner or lost. The condition of the dust jacket should be graded independently of the book. It's also worth noting that many of the early strip reprint comics were printed in hardcover with dust jackets.

Special thanks to John K. Snyder, Jr., Russ Cochran, Denis Kitchen, and Marc Nathan

A tabloid-sized edition of the **Acme Novelty Library** series by Chris Ware, published by Fantagraphics Books.

Comic Book Certification: An Overview of Comics Guaranty, LLC

by Steve Borock

*EDITORIAL NOTE: Since entering the comic book market in 2000, CGC has provided independent, third party grading services for comic books utilizing standards put forth in this volume, its predecessor, and **The Overstreet Comic Book Price Guide**. While this by no means precludes the sale of comics through traditional means and circumstances, the availability of this service has greatly enhanced the attractiveness of comics, particularly those at the high end, as long-term investments.*

Comics Guaranty, LLC (CGC) opened for business in January of 2000 and quickly became an integral part of the way buyers and sellers do business; this is particularly true of internet transactions. CGC is an expert and impartial third-party grading service, one of three independent companies operating under the umbrella of the Certified Collectibles Group, LLC (CCG). As with the other CCG companies, Numismatic Guaranty Corporation (NGC) and Sportscard Guaranty, LLC (SGC), CGC employs the brightest and most ethical individuals in the comics field. These are persons fully qualified to grade comics while checking for authenticity and detecting restoration that can affect a book's value. This critical information is defined on the CGC label, which is then encapsulated in CGC's inner well along with the book. Such a level of protection, and the confidence it affords to both buyer and seller, have long since revolutionized the coin and card fields. Now, with the establishment of CGC, this protection is available to the comic book enthusiast.

Initially, the CGC principals consulted many of the most respected individuals in our hobby, and based on their recommendations they selected the initial team of graders. Once the core grading team was in place, CGC began the development of its revolutionary tamper-evident holder. This proved to be quite a technical challenge - many designs were rejected before the perfect combination of materials and design was found. A significant amount of time, energy and capital went into perfecting our current holder.

No less challenging was the establishment of a uniform grading standard that would meet the expectations of knowledgeable buyers and sellers. While everyone seemed to agree that the Overstreet reference was the foundation of this standard, there were a number of subjective interpretations of its published definitions. CGC understood from our inception that this was just a starting point; it was still necessary to take a consensus from the day-to-day experience of the nation's top dealers and collectors. This was achieved by inviting 50 of the hobby's top experts to undertake a grueling, hours long grading test. From this, CGC developed a median standard that reflects the collective knowledge of these prominent figures.

Many thousands of comics are submitted each month to CGC by persons who have confidence in our consistency and integrity as a grading service. It's likely that little thought is given by these submitters to the exact process by which their comics are graded and encapsulated, since they're pleased with the value received. In actual fact, the process involves numerous steps within several specialized departments, all of which have as their ultimate role the expeditious processing of a "raw" (uncertified) comic into one which is accurately graded and sonically sealed inside a CGC holder. It's quite a team effort, and you're invited to follow along as we trace the progress of a comic through the process of certification at CGC.

Submitting Comics to CGC

Typically, comics received by CGC are submitted through one of our authorized member-dealers, each of whom has passed a thorough background check by CGC's Accounting and Customer Service departments. This ensures that a customer's comic is in reliable hands when it's being prepared for shipment to CGC's offices in Florida. The value of such a precaution is self-evident, but it also relieves the collector or investor from having to provide personal and financial information which he or she may wish to keep confidential. Another option for individuals who wish to submit comics directly to CGC is to become a member of the Certified Collectors Society. Such membership provides for direct submission to any one of the three companies comprising the Certified Collectibles Group, as well as offering numerous other benefits.

Pre-printed submission invoices are provided to all of CGC's authorized member-dealers. The member-dealer who handles a customer's submission keeps the bottom copy of each invoice as a record of the comics being sent to CGC. Included on the invoice is the submitter's declaration of each book's value. This is important information to

Human Torch #2 (#1), Timely, 1940. CGC VF+ 8.5, off-white pages.

have in the unlikely event of a package being lost while in transit. Comics are typically sent to CGC's offices by registered post or through an insured express company.

The Comics Are Received

CGC's Receiving Department opens the newly arrived packages each morning and immediately verifies that the number of books in each package matches the number shown on the invoice. Once this is done, a more detailed comparison is made to ensure that their invoice descriptions correspond to the actual comics. This information is entered into a computer, and the comics will thenceforth be traceable at all stages of the grading process by their invoice number and their line number within that invoice. Each book is placed within protective Mylar that has affixed to it a label bearing the invoice and line item numbers, information which is duplicated on the label in a barcoded inscription for quick reading by the computer. Before any grading is performed, each book is examined by CGC's Restoration Detection Expert. If any form of restoration work is detected, he enters this information into the computer so that it will be available to the grading team.

The Grading Process

After being examined by

More Fun Comics #54 (Larson), DC, 1940. CGC VF/NM 9.0, off-white to white pages.

New Comics #1,
DC, 1935. CGC FN/VF 7.0,
cream to off-white pages.

there is disagreement among the graders, a discussion will ensue until a final determination is made and the book forwarded.

Encapsulating the Comics

After each comic has been graded and the necessary numbers and text entered into their respective data fields, all the comics on a particular invoice are taken from the Grading Department into the Encapsulation Department. Here, appropriately color-coded labels are printed out bearing the appropriate descriptive text, including each book's grade and identification number. This last item is extremely important, as it serves to make each certified comic unique and is also an important deterrent to the counterfeiting of CGC's valued product. All of the above information is duplicated in a bar code, which appears underneath the written text on the comic's label.

The newly-printed labels are stacked in the same sequence as the comics to be encapsulated with them, ensuring that each book and its label match one another. The comic is now ready to be fitted inside an archival-quality inte-

the Restoration Detection Expert, a book then passes to a pre-grader, who counts the number of pages and enters into the computer any peculiarities or flaws that may affect grading. Some examples of this would be "a tear on third page," "a corner crease – does not break color," "a 1/2" inch spine split," and so forth. He then enters this information, if necessary, into the "Graders Notes" field and assigns his grading opinion. When the next grader examines the comic, he is not able to see the first person's assigned grade, so as to not influence his own evaluation. After determining his own grade for the comic, he can then view the Graders Notes entered by the previous grader, and he may add to this commentary if he believes more remarks are in order. This same process is repeated as the comic passes to the Grading Finalizer. He makes a final restoration check before determining his own grade, at which time he then reviews the grades and notes entered by the previous graders. If all grades are in agreement or are very close, he will then assign the book's final grade. The comic is then forwarded to the Encapsulation Department for sealing. If

More Fun Comics #73 (Mile High), DC, 1941. CGC NM 9.4, white pages.

Planet Comics #1,
Fiction House, 1940. CGC NM 9.4,
off-white pages.

Silver Streak Comics #6,
Lev Gleason, 1940. CGC NM- 9.2,
cream to off-white pages.

rior well, which is then sealed within a transparent capsule, along with the book's color-coded label. This is accomplished through a combination of compression and ultrasonic vibration. The result is a newly-encapsulated CGC comic, ready to be shipped to its proud owner.

The Comics Are Shipped

After encapsulation, all comics are returned briefly to the Grading Department for a quality control inspection. Here, they are examined to make certain that their labels are correct for both the grade and its accompanying descriptive information. The quality control person also inspects each book for any flaws in its holder, such as scuffs or nicks. While these are quite rare, CGC is careful to make certain that the comics it certifies are not only accurately graded but attractively presented as well.

When all the comics have been inspected, they're either held in CGC's vault for in-person pick-up by the submitter or delivered to our Shipping Department for packaging. As in all steps of the grading process, the comics are counted and their labels checked against the

original hand-written or typed invoice to make certain that no mistakes have occurred. A Shipping Department employee then verifies the method of transport as selected by the submitter on the invoice and prepares the comics for delivery.

No matter whether the U. S. Postal Service or some private carrier is used, the method of packaging is essentially the same. The encapsulated comics are placed vertically inside boxes made of very sturdy cardboard, and these boxes contain a row of dividers so that the capsules don't come into contact with one another. A shipping copy of the submitter's invoice is included before the box is sealed and heavy tape is used to prevent accidental or unauthorized opening of the box while it's in transit.

The CGC Label

Comic books certified by CGC bear color-coded labels that have different meanings. Whenever purchasing a CGC-certified comic, be certain to note not just the book's grade but also its label category. A Universal label is denoted by the color blue and indicates that a book was not found to have any qualifying defects or signs of restoration. There is one exception to this policy: At CGC's discretion, comics having a very minor amount of glue and/or color touch-up may still qualify for a Universal label provided that they were from 1950 or earlier and that such restoration is noted underneath the assigned grade. The above description also applies to CGC's red Modern label, now discontinued.

As its name implies, the Restored label, identified by the color purple, is used for books found to have restoration work performed on them. The grade assigned is based on the book's appearance, with the restoration noted. A distinction is made between Amateur and Professional restoration, this judgment being based on the materials used. Since the degree of work performed is also significant with restored books, there are a total of seven possible descriptions under the Restored label. Each description is prefaced with the word Apparent, followed by Slight, Moderate or Extensive in combination with the final descriptors Amateur or Professional. Examples of Restored labels might read Apparent Moderate Professional or Apparent Slight Amateur, both descriptions then

being followed by the book's grade. Finally, comics which have had no restoration other than a trimming of their covers or edges are labeled as simply Apparent, followed by their grade.

The Qualified label is green, and this indicates that one qualifying defect is present on a book. An example of such a qualifying feature would be a missing Marvel Value Stamp that does not affect the story. While such a book technically may grade Fair 1.0, it may appear to grade Near Mint+ 9.6. In such instances, assigning a grade of just 1.0 does not fully represent the value of the comic to a collector. Through use of the green Qualified label, a comic buyer is able to make an informed decision as to what he is purchasing in terms of its overall desirability. Because of the complexity involved, green labels are assigned quite seldom and then only when considered absolutely necessary. In addition, comic books that have a signature and that do not fall under the Signature Series label get the Qualified label. This is the most common use for the Qualified label. This shows what the grade of the book would have been if the signature was not present.

CGC's Signature Series label is yellow, and this is used when CGC's policy of determining that a signature is authentic has been met. The yellow label includes the grade before a comic was signed, who signed it, and when it was signed. If appropriate and when known, a Signature Series label may state at which venue a book was signed.

A Proven Standard of Integrity

CGC employees are not allowed to engage in the commercial buying or selling of comics. In this way, CGC can remain completely impartial, having no vested interest other than a devotion to serving clients through accurate and consistent grading.

For more information on comic book certification and CGC's many services, please visit our website at www.CGCcomics.com.

Showcase #4,
DC, 1956. CGC VF 8.0,
off-white pages.

Special thanks to Heritage Comics for the use of their photographs from "The Nicolas Cage Collection."

Using The 10 Point Grading Scale

The following grade descriptions use both the traditional nomenclature and grade abbreviations - with the exception of the newly designated Gem Mint (GM) - as well as the numerical equivalent on the Overstreet 10 Point Comic Book Grading Scale.

Please note that we have tried to be as exhaustive as possible within the space available when listing the many defects that can occur within the various grades. This does *not* mean that all listed defects are allowed within each grade *simultaneously*. Each grade will likely exhibit *some* combination of the allowable defects, and the final grade depends on the number of defects present and their relative severity. For example, some defects may be more extreme for a particular grade as long as other acceptable listed defects are almost non-existent.

Policy on Plus/Minus Grades

All of the grades on the 10 Point scale have been given their own section, with explanatory notes and a table of allowable defects, *except for the plus/minus grades from VF+ and below*. Comic books that are graded with either a plus or a minus grade fit all of the criteria for the primary grade in question, with one specific defect or small accumulation of defects - or a comparable number of virtues - that, respectively, limit or heighten the book's value beyond that of the major grade. In almost all such cases, it is the cumulative effect on the eye appeal of the book that determines whether or not a comic shifts from a primary grade (for example, Very Fine) to a plus or minus grade (either Very Fine + or Very Fine -).

Number of Allowable Defects

The accompanying chart provides some idea of the estimated number of accumulated defects allowed for each grade. Please remember that quantity of defects is only part of the story. For example, a book with two or three minor defects may grade significantly higher than a book with one very severe defect.

On Generalized Terminology

Throughout the grade descriptions and tables of allowable defects, the Grading Guide employs a number of modifying adjectives like "minor," "moderate" and "severe" to describe a wide range of comic book conditions. Given the subjective nature of comic book grading, we do not wish to set all such determining factors in stone - nor, indeed, could we if we wanted to - but we do want to give all comic book graders a generalized sense of what is allowable in any given grade.

We do understand that such vague terms could be frustrating, so to further clarify the use

10 Point Grading Scale		
10.0	GM	Gem Mint
9.9	MT	Mint
9.8	NM/MT	Near Mint/Mint
9.6	NM+	Near Mint+
9.4	NM	Near Mint
9.2	NM-	Near Mint-
9.0	VF/NM	Very Fine/Near Mint
8.5	VF+	Very Fine+
8.0	VF	Very Fine
7.5	VF-	Very Fine-
7.0	FN/VF	Fine/Very Fine
6.5	FN+	Fine+
6.0	FN	Fine
5.5	FN-	Fine-
5.0	VG/FN	Very Good/Fine
4.5	VG+	Very Good+
4.0	VG	Very Good
3.5	VG-	Very Good-
3.0	GD/VG	Good/Very Good
2.5	GD+	Good+
2.0	GD	Good
1.8	GD-	Good-
1.5	FR/GD	Fair/Good
1.0	FR	Fair
0.5	PR	Poor

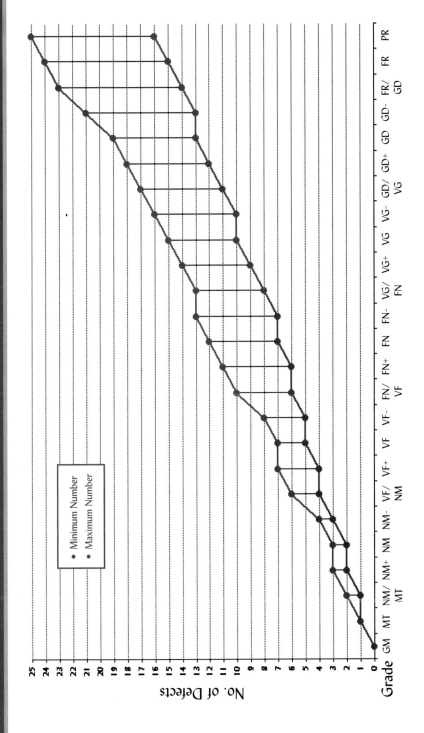

Suggested Number of Allowable Defects per Grade

127

of such terminology, we offer a brief guide on the page following the allowable defects chart to the kinds of measurements and/or quantities that may be implied by these terms. Please note that as with all such material in this volume, these are only guidelines and do not necessarily apply to all cases.

Obviously, combinations of these generalized terms are also used to describe certain aspects of a grade, and in those cases, you might consult this list to see what measurement and quantity ranges might apply. For example, a comic book in Fine/Very Fine 7.0 is allowed "some accumulation of minor defects" under the category "Bindery/Printing Defects." Consulting the ranges below, this could mean that such a comic might have 4-6 related defects of no more than 1/4" in size or length. This could include an 1/8" white area on the front cover near the spine (where the back cover has wrapped around to the front), a diagonal miscut of the cover, a vertical miscut that has resulted in 1/16" of the front cover removed from the bottom, and/or a 1/8" bindery tear in the top right corner.

Paper Quality - What is "White?"

While we continue to use familiar terminology in describing interior paper quality, such as "white," "off-white," "cream," and so on, we must qualify our use of the word "white." Due to the wildly diverse paper stocks employed by the various comic book publishers over the years, the highest possible color quality of the paper in a given comic book may differ markedly from that of another comic from another company or era. Therefore, we use the term "white" loosely in all cases to refer to the highest quality color and freshness of the paper stock used in any given comic regardless of the actual color that may be evident. Subsequent descriptions of "off-white," "cream," "tan" and others should then be interpreted in relation to the "white" starting point of any given book.

Pedigree Books

As many collectors already know, there are a group of special comic books, usually referred to as "pedigrees," that represent the most exceptional examples of an issue or title - in fact, many agree that a book from one of these collections could very well be one of, if not the only, best surviving copies of a given book. Pedigree books have high cover gloss, brilliant cover inks and white, fresh, supple pages that place them far above other books that might receive the same technical grade. Books from these pedigree collections, therefore, actually transcend their technical grade. Of these, many collectors and dealers agree that the most important collections are the Mile High (Edgar Church) collection, the San Francisco (Reilly) collection, and the Gaines file copies, but there are of course many others. The striking difference between a regular copy of a particular issue and a pedigree copy becomes apparent when comparing two such examples in the same basic grade. In most cases, the pedigree book will far outshine the generic one.

	TERM	INDIV. DEFECT	QTY OF DEFECTS
SUGGESTED RANGES OF MEASUREMENT/QUANTITY	slight, subtle	1/32" to 1/16"	1
	small	1/16" to 1/8"	1-2
	limited accumulation		2-4
	very minor	1/16" to 1/8"	2-5
	few		3-5
	minor, minimal	1/8" to 1/4"	3-5
	some accumulation		4-6
	moderate	1/4" to 1"	4-8
	small accumulation		4-8
	considerable, significant	1" and up	8-10
	many, accumulation		8-16
	extensive, extreme	2-3" and up	10-25

Other Defects

The grade descriptions attempt to provide an overall view of the defects that can come into play throughout the scale. There are, of course, many other defects that are not mentioned specifically within those descriptions, but are just as important in determining grade. While these additional defects, such as dust shadows and pin holes, may not be discussed in the grade descriptions themselves - not for any qualitative reason but more for a simple lack of space - they are at the very least either illustrated by examples shown throughout the book or described in the glossary. In the case of creator autographs and owner signatures, we suggest that such inscriptions might not be considered a defect in any book graded Mint (9.9) and below. As for the question of transparent covers, there does not seem to be any appreciable affect on grade when that particular defect is present according to many experts, although it has inspired some debate as to whether the impact of a transparent cover on a comic book's grade should be re-evaluated in the future.

One other caveat: in many of our grade descriptions, we might say "tears are common" or "book-length creases are allowed." Many of our descriptions make use of the plural tense when referring to various individual grades. While an accumulation of a particular defect may indeed be allowed within a given grade, the use of the plural tense in describing certain defects is not necessarily indicative of the presence of multiple defects, but merely a grammatical choice indicating that a given defect is allowed in all of the comics that fall within that grade.

As you can see, while we have tried to quantify some aspects of comic book grading to aid understanding and provide a set of standards for all collectors to follow, for practical purposes we have left many areas intentionally open to interpretation. Ultimately, the grade of an individual comic book must be decided by human observers.

Diagram of a Comic Book

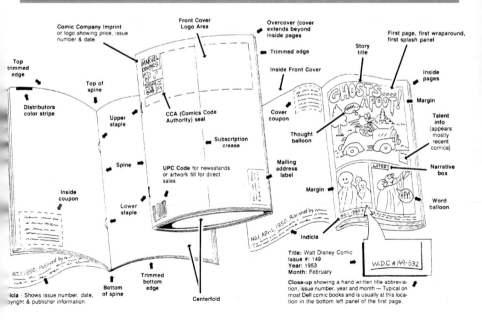

(10.0) GEM MINT (GM)

GRADE DESCRIPTION:
This is an exceptional example of a given book - the best ever seen. The slightest bindery defects and/or printing flaws may be seen only upon very close inspection.

The overall look is "as if it has never been handled or released for purchase."

BINDERY/PRINTING DEFECTS - Only the slightest bindery or printing defects are allowed, and these would be imperceptible on first viewing. No bindery tears.

COVER/EXTERIOR - Flat with no surface wear. Inks are bright with high reflectivity. Well centered and firmly secured to interior pages. Corners are cut square and sharp. No creases. No dates or stamped markings allowed. No soiling, staining or other discoloration.

SPINE - Tight and flat. No spine roll or split allowed.

STAPLES - Must be original, centered and clean with no rust. No staple tears or stress lines.

PAPER/INTERIOR - Paper is white, supple and fresh. No hint of acidity in the odor of the newsprint. No interior autographs or owner signatures. Centerfold is firmly secure. No interior tears.

Collectors should thoroughly examine any book listed as 10.0. These books should also be carefully scrutinized for restoration.

BINDERY/PRINTING
only the slightest,
most imperceptible defects

COVER INKS/GLOSS
bright with high reflectivity

COVER WEAR
flat, no wear,
well centered, secure

COVER CREASES
none allowed

SOILING, STAINING
none allowed

DATES/STAMPS
none allowed

SPINE ROLL
tight and flat, no roll

SPINE SPLIT
none allowed

STAPLES
original, centered, clean

STAPLE TEARS
none allowed

RUST MIGRATION
none allowed

STRESS LINES
none allowed

CORNERS
sharp, square, no creases

CENTERFOLD
firmly secure

INTERIOR TEARS
none allowed

PAPER QUALITY/COLOR
white, supple and fresh

ACID ODOR
none allowed

MISSING PIECES
none allowed

AMATEUR REPAIRS
none allowed

COUPON CUT
none allowed

READABILITY
preserved

GM

Green Arrow #137, October 1998. © DC Comics.
Obvious defects: None.
Hidden defects: None.
OWL: 10.

Spine is flat
and tight

Sharp
corners

Firmly
secure
center-
fold

No corner
abrasion

No edge tears or
creases

Wolverine: The Origin #1, November 2001. © Marvel Characters Inc.
Obvious defects: None.
Hidden defects: None.
OWL: 10.

Sharp
corners

Bright reflectivity
on cover

Spine is flat
and tight

Colors are
brilliant

The Ultimates #1, March 2002. © Marvel Characters Inc.
Obvious defects: None.
Hidden defects: None.
OWL: 10.

Sharp
corners

Spine is tight
and flat

Inks have high
reflectivity

Star Wars: Episode II - Attack of the Clones #1, April 2002. © Lucasfilm Ltd.
Obvious defects: None.
Hidden defects: None.
OWL: 10.

Sharp
corners

No corner
abrasion

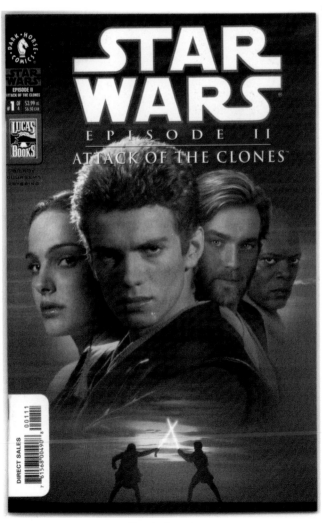

No edge tears or
creases

Transformers: Generation One #1, April 2002. © Hasbro.
Obvious defects: None.
Hidden defects: None.
OWL: Not applicable.

Sharp
corners

No creases or
wear on edges

GM

Birds of Prey #41, May 2002. © DC Comics.
Obvious defects: None.
Hidden defects: None.
OWL: 10.

Sharp
corners

Bright colors

Tight
spine

Inks have high
reflectivity

(9.9) MINT (MT)

MT

GRADE DESCRIPTION:
Near perfect in every way.

The overall look is "as if it was just purchased from the news-stand."

BINDERY DEFECTS - Only subtle bindery or printing defects are allowed. No bindery tears.

COVER/EXTERIOR - Flat with no surface wear. Inks are bright with high reflectivity and minimal fading. Generally well centered and firmly secured to interior pages. Corners are cut square and sharp. No creases. Small, inconspicuous, lightly penciled, stamped or inked arrival dates are acceptable as long as they are in an unobtrusive location. No soiling, staining or other discoloration.

SPINE - Tight and flat. No spine roll or split allowed.

STAPLES - Must be original, generally centered and clean with no rust. No staple tears or stress lines.

PAPER/INTERIOR - Paper is white, supple and fresh. No hint of acidity in the odor of the newsprint. Centerfold is firmly secure. No interior tears.

Comics published before 1970 in MINT condition are extremely scarce.

MT

BINDERY/PRINTING
only subtle defects,
no bindery tears

COVER INKS/GLOSS
bright with high reflectivity

COVER WEAR
flat, no wear,
well centered, secure

COVER CREASES
none allowed

SOILING, STAINING
none allowed

DATES/STAMPS
small, inconspicuous
dates/initials allowed

SPINE ROLL
tight and flat, no roll

SPINE SPLIT
none allowed

STAPLES
original, clean,
generally centered

STAPLE TEARS
none allowed

RUST MIGRATION
none allowed

STRESS LINES
none allowed

CORNERS
sharp, square, no creases

CENTERFOLD
firmly secure

INTERIOR TEARS
none allowed

PAPER QUALITY/COLOR
white, supple and fresh

ACID ODOR
none allowed

MISSING PIECES
none allowed

AMATEUR REPAIRS
none allowed

COUPON CUT
none allowed

READABILITY
preserved

MT

Zip Comics #7, August 1940. © MLJ Magazines.
Edgar Church (Mile High) pedigree copy.
Obvious defects: None.
Hidden defects: None.
OWL: 10.
Note: This is the first Golden Age comic graded as a Mint 9.9 by CGC.

Slightest
bindery
defect in
corner

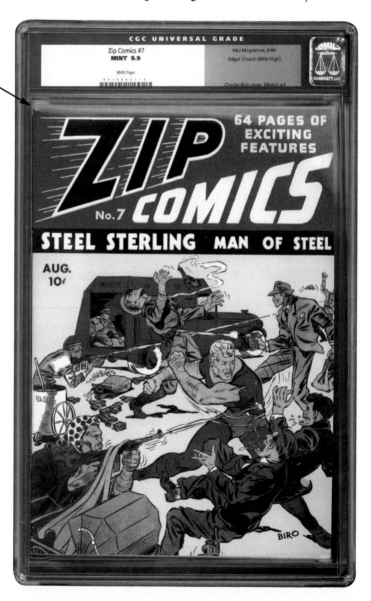

The Flash #147, September 1964. © DC Comics.
Obvious defects: Slight fading of cover inks.
Hidden defects: None.
OWL: 10.

Spine is flat
and tight

Slight fading
on edge

Sharp
corners

No corner
abrasion

No edge tears or
creases

MT

The Authority #14, June 2000. © WildStorm Productions.
Obvious defects: None.
Hidden defects: Small color fleck.
OWL: 10.

Color
fleck

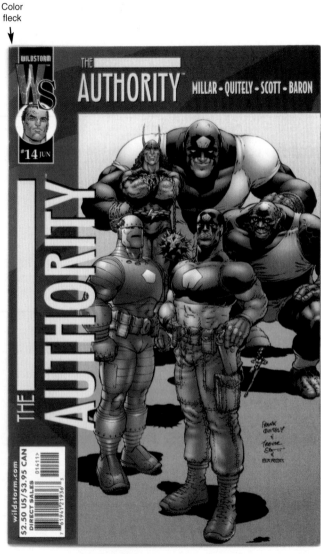

Inks have high
reflectivity

Fray #1, June 2001. © Joss Whedon.
Obvious defects: Bindery defect - slightly miswrapped cover.
Hidden defects: None.
OWL: 10.

MT

Cover slightly
miswrapped

MT

Batman: The 10-cent Adventure, March 2002. © DC Comics.
Obvious defects: Very subtle bend near spine.
Hidden defects: None.
OWL: 10.

Sharp
corners

Very
subtle
bend

No edge tears or
creases

The Incredible Hulk Vol. 2 #38, May 2002. © Marvel Characters Inc.
Obvious defects: Printing defect - small ink blotch.
Hidden defects: None.
OWL: 10.

MT

Small ink
blotch
behind
Hulk's
neck

(9.8) NEAR MINT/MINT (NM/MT)

GRADE DESCRIPTION:
Nearly perfect in every way with only minor imperfections that keep it from the next higher grade.

The overall look is "as if it was just purchased from the newsstand."

BINDERY DEFECTS - Only subtle bindery or printing defects are allowed. No bindery tears.

COVER/EXTERIOR - Flat with no surface wear. Inks are bright with high reflectivity and minimal fading. Generally well centered and firmly secured to interior pages. Corners are cut square and sharp. No creases. Small, inconspicuous, lightly penciled, stamped or inked arrival dates are acceptable as long as they are in an unobtrusive location. No soiling, staining or other discoloration.

SPINE - Tight and flat. No spine roll or split allowed.

STAPLES - Must be original, generally centered and clean with no rust. No staple tears or stress lines.

PAPER/INTERIOR - Paper is white, supple and fresh. No hint of acidity in the odor of the newsprint. Centerfold is firmly secure. Only the slightest interior tears are allowed.

NM/MT

BINDERY/PRINTING
only subtle, no bindery tears

COVER INKS/GLOSS
bright with high reflectivity

COVER WEAR
flat, no wear, well centered

COVER CREASES
none allowed

SOILING, STAINING
none allowed

DATES/STAMPS
small, inconspicuous
dates/initials allowed

SPINE ROLL
tight and flat, no roll

SPINE SPLIT
none allowed

STAPLES
original, clean,
generally centered

STAPLE TEARS
none allowed

RUST MIGRATION
none allowed

STRESS LINES
none allowed

CORNERS
sharp, square, no creases

CENTERFOLD
firmly secure

INTERIOR TEARS
slightest tears allowed

PAPER QUALITY/COLOR
white, supple and fresh

ACID ODOR
none allowed

MISSING PIECES
none allowed

AMATEUR REPAIRS
none allowed

COUPON CUT
none allowed

READABILITY
preserved

Crackajack Funnies #1, June, 1938. © Dell Publishing Co.
Edgar Church (Mile High) pedigree copy.
Obvious defects: None.
Hidden defects: None.
OWL: 10.

NM/MT

All corners are sharp

Pencilled arrival date
does not affect grade

Cover
slightly mis-
wrapped

Slight
oxidation
shadow

Grease
pencilled
number

Mad #1, October-November 1956. © EC Publications.
Gaines file copy.
Obvious defects: None.
Hidden defects: None.
OWL: 10.

Very subtle
bindery cut

All corners are sharp. This book has
one or two almost imperceptible flaws.

Witchblade #2, January, 1996. © Top Cow Productions, Inc.
Obvious defects: None.
Hidden defects: Slight fading of cover inks.
OWL: Not applicable.

NM/MT

Color
fleck

Corner
color
fleck

Daredevil Volume 2 #1, November 1998. © Marvel Characters, Inc.
Obvious defects: Tiny color flecks along gatefold front cover.
Hidden defects: None.
OWL: Not applicable.

Color
fleck

Color
fleck

Gatefold
cover

The Dark Knight Strikes Again #1, 2001. © DC Comics.
Obvious defects: None.
Hidden defects: Small color fleck.
OWL: 10.

Color
fleck

Small color
fleck in corner

G. I. Joe #1, 2001. © Hasbro.
Obvious defects: None.
Hidden defects: Very slight interior tear. Color fleck on back cover.
OWL: 10.

Corners are
perfect

Color
fleck

(9.6) **NEAR MINT+** (NM+)

GRADE DESCRIPTION:
Nearly perfect with a minor additional virtue or virtues that raise it from Near Mint. The overall look is "as if it was just purchased from the newsstand and read once or twice."

BINDERY DEFECTS - Only subtle bindery or printing defects are allowed. No bindery tears are allowed, although on Golden Age books bindery tears of up to 1/8" have been noted.

COVER/EXTERIOR - Flat with no surface wear. Inks are bright with high reflectivity and a minimum of fading. Well centered and firmly secured to interior pages. One corner may be almost imperceptibly blunted, but still almost sharp and cut square. Almost imperceptible indentations are permissible, but no creases, bends, or color break. Small, inconspicuous, lightly penciled, stamped or inked arrival dates are acceptable as long as they are in an unobtrusive location. No soiling, staining or other discoloration.

SPINE - Tight and flat. No spine roll or split allowed.

STAPLES - Must be original, generally centered, with only the slightest discoloration. No staple tears, stress lines, or rust migration.

PAPER/INTERIOR - Paper is off-white, supple and fresh. No hint of acidity in the odor of the newsprint. Centerfold is firmly secure. Only the slightest interior tears are allowed.

BINDERY/PRINTING

only subtle, no tears on Silver Age
and later, 1/8" on Golden Age

COVER INKS/GLOSS

bright with high reflectivity

COVER WEAR

flat, no wear, well centered

COVER CREASES

almost imperceptible indentations
allowed

SOILING, STAINING

none allowed

DATES/STAMPS

small, inconspicuous
dates/initials allowed

NM+

SPINE ROLL

tight and flat, no roll

SPINE SPLIT

none allowed

STAPLES

original, generally cen-
tered, slight discoloration

STAPLE TEARS

none allowed

RUST MIGRATION

none allowed

STRESS LINES

none allowed

CORNERS

almost sharp, one imperceptible
blunted corner allowed

CENTERFOLD

firmly secure

INTERIOR TEARS

slightest tears allowed

PAPER QUALITY/COLOR

off-white, supple and fresh

ACID ODOR

none allowed

MISSING PIECES

none allowed

AMATEUR REPAIRS

none allowed

COUPON CUT

none allowed

READABILITY

preserved

More Fun Comics #59, September 1940. © DC Comics.
Obvious defects: Oxidation shadow. Pencil marks and color fleck.
Hidden defects: None.
OWL: 9.

Very light
oxidation
shadow

NM+

Pencil
marks

Very small
color fleck

Ibis The Invincible #1, January 1942. © Fawcett Publications.
Obvious defects: Light pencil marks in upper corners.
Hidden defects: None.
OWL: 9.

Pencil marks

Pencil mark

Very minor blunted corner

NM+

Very light stress line at spine on back cover

Crime Patrol #15, Dec. 1949-Jan 1950. © William M. Gaines.
Obvious defects: None.
Hidden defects: None.
OWL: 8.

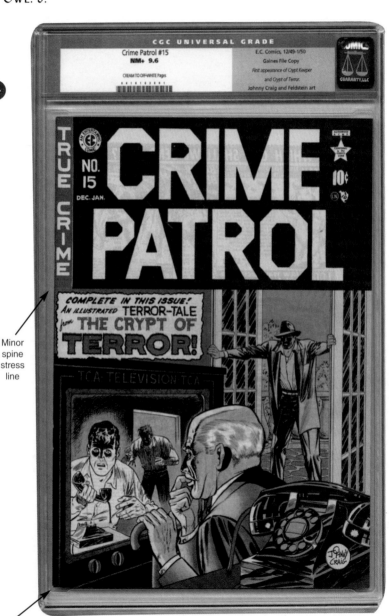

Minor
spine
stress
line

Very minor
blunted corner

The Crypt of Terror #17, April-May 1950. © William M. Gaines.
Obvious defects: None.
Hidden defects: None.
OWL: 9.

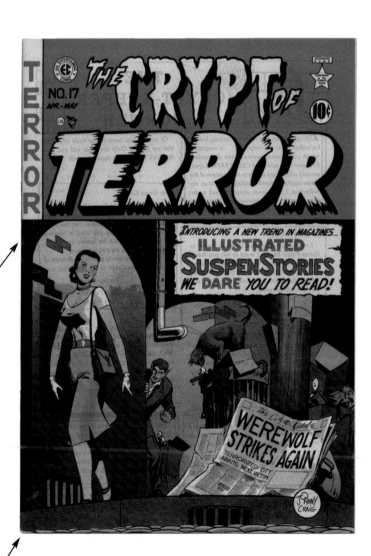

NM+

Minor
spine
stress
line

Very minor
blunted corner

Incredible Hulk #181, November 1974. © Marvel Characters, Inc.
Obvious defects: None.
Hidden defects: Minor color flecking.
OWL: 10.

Minor blunted
corner

Sharp
corner

NM+

Slight
indentation
on cover

Minor edge
stress

Uncanny X-Men #207, July 1986. © Marvel Characters, Inc.
Obvious defects: None.
Hidden defects: None.
OWL: 10.

Minor corner
abrasion

Small
indentation

NM+

Walt Disney's Mickey Mouse #250, September 1989. © Walt Disney Company.
Obvious defects: None.
Hidden defects: None.
OWL: 9.

Minor corner abrasion

Small indentation

NM+

Minor stress line

Strangers in Paradise Vol. 3 #1, October 1996. © Terry Moore.
Obvious defects: None.
Hidden defects: None.
OWL: 10.

NM+

Small
indentation

Minor corner
abrasion

(9.4) NEAR MINT (NM)

NM

GRADE DESCRIPTION:
Nearly perfect with only minor imperfections that keep it from the next higher grade. The overall look is "as if it was just purchased from the newsstand and read once or twice."

BINDERY DEFECTS - Subtle defects are allowed. Bindery tears must be less than 1/16" on Silver Age and later books, although on Golden Age books bindery tears of up to 1/4" have been noted.

COVER/EXTERIOR - Flat with no surface wear. Inks are bright with high reflectivity and a minimum of fading. Generally well centered and secured to interior pages. Corners are cut square and sharp with ever-so-slight blunting permitted. A 1/16" bend is permitted with no color break. No creases. Small, inconspicuous, lightly penciled, stamped or inked arrival dates are acceptable as long as they are in an unobtrusive location. No soiling, staining or other discoloration apart from slight foxing.

SPINE - Tight and flat. No spine roll or split allowed.

STAPLES - Generally centered; may have slight discoloration. No staple tears are allowed; almost no stress lines. No rust migration. In rare cases, a comic was not stapled at the bindery and therefore has a missing staple; this is not considered a defect. Any staple can be replaced on books up to Fine, but only vintage staples can be used on books from Very Fine to Near Mint. Mint books must have original staples.

PAPER/INTERIOR - Paper is off-white to cream, supple and fresh. No hint of acidity in the odor of the newsprint. Centerfold is secure. Slight interior tears are allowed.

Comics published before 1970 in NEAR MINT condition are scarce. This grade is commonly viewed by the average collector as the best grade obtainable.

Collectors should thoroughly examine these books for restoration, particularly in the case of pre-1965 books. Expensive and key books listed as being in "high grade" frequently have some restoration. In most cases, restoration performed on otherwise NEAR MINT books will reduce the grade. A VERY FINE comic book cannot be transformed into a NEAR MINT comic book through restoration.

BINDERY/PRINTING

subtle, tears up to 1/16" on Silver Age and later, 1/4" on Golden Age

COVER INKS/GLOSS

bright with high reflectivity

COVER WEAR

flat, no wear, generally centered, secure

COVER CREASES

1/16" bend with no color break allowed

SOILING, STAINING

none allowed except for slight foxing

DATES/STAMPS

small, inconspicuous dates/initials allowed

NM

SPINE ROLL

tight and flat, no roll

SPINE SPLIT

none allowed

STAPLES

generally centered, slight discoloration

STAPLE TEARS

none allowed

RUST MIGRATION

none allowed

STRESS LINES

almost no lines

CORNERS

ever-so-slight blunting, no creases

CENTERFOLD

secure

INTERIOR TEARS

slight tears allowed

PAPER QUALITY/COLOR

off-white/cream, supple and fresh

ACID ODOR

none allowed

MISSING PIECES

none allowed

AMATEUR REPAIRS

none allowed

COUPON CUT

none allowed

READABILITY

preserved

Nickel Comics #1, May 1940. © Fawcett Publications.
Obvious defects: Lower left corner chip.
Hidden defects: Subtle color flecks.
OWL: 8.

Corner
fleck

Color
flecks

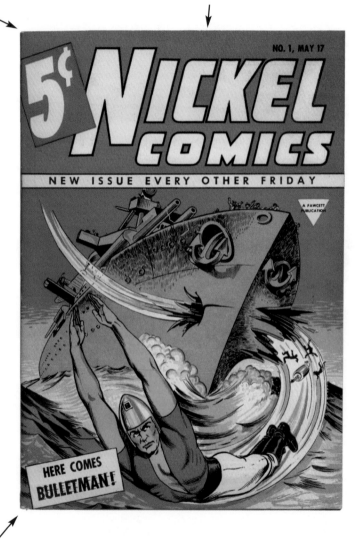

NM

Corner
chip

All-Flash Quarterly #1, Summer 1941. © DC Comics.
Obvious defects: Slight abrasion in upper right corner.
Hidden defects: None.
OWL: **8**.

Corner
chip

NM

Copy
originally
not
stapled

Spine
stress
line

Slight
foxing

Daredevil Comics #1, July 1941. © Lev Gleason Publications.
Obvious defects: Very minor bindery tear.
Hidden defects: None.
OWL: 8.

Very minor
bindery tear

NM

Minor
indentation

Minor corner
wear

Marvel Mystery Comics #65, July 1945. © Marvel Characters, Inc.
Obvious defects: Small tear on lower left corner.
Hidden defects: None.
OWL: 8.

Browning on edge

Pencil marks

NM

Small corner tear

Slight edge wear

169

Atomic Comics #2, March 1946. © Green Publishing Co.
Obvious defects: Cover stamp.
Hidden defects: Minor inconspicuous staining.
OWL: 8.
Note: Cover printed on non-glossy paper. Cover stamp is sufficiently inconspicuous.

Minor
corner wear

Minor
corner fleck

NM

Cover
stamp

Minor
indentation

The Avengers #141, November 1975. © Marvel Characters, Inc.
Obvious defects: None.
Hidden defects: Very minor color fleck.
OWL: 9.

NM

Slight
indentation

Color
fleck

Color
fleck

Marvel Two-In-One #50, April 1979. © Marvel Characters, Inc.
Obvious defects: None.
Hidden defects: None.
OWL: **8**.

Corner not
squarely cut

Slight
staining

Abraded
corner

Amazing Spider-Man Vol. 2 #36, December 2001. © Marvel Characters, Inc.
Obvious defects: Minor corner crease.
Hidden defects: Very minute color flecking on the all black area. Some flecks are
known to be printer defects and should not be color-touched.
OWL: 10.

1/16" bend

Sharp
corner

NM

Minute
color
flecks

Minor
chip

Very minor
corner
crease

(9.2) **NEAR MINT-** (NM-)

GRADE DESCRIPTION:
Nearly perfect with only a minor additional defect or defects that keep it from Near Mint. The overall look is "as if it was just purchased from the newsstand and read once or twice."

NM-

BINDERY DEFECTS - A limited number of minor defects are allowed.

COVER/EXTERIOR - Flat with no surface wear. Inks are bright with only the slightest dimming of reflectivity. Generally well centered and secured to interior pages. Corners are cut square and sharp with ever-so-slight blunting permitted. A 1/16-1/8" bend is permitted with no color break. No creases. Small, inconspicuous, lightly penciled, stamped or inked arrival dates are acceptable as long as they are in an unobtrusive location. No soiling, staining or other discoloration apart from slight foxing.

SPINE - Tight and flat. No spine roll or split allowed.

STAPLES - May show some discoloration. No staple tears are allowed; almost no stress lines. No rust migration. In rare cases, a comic was not stapled at the bindery and therefore has a missing staple; this is not considered a defect. Any staple can be replaced on books up to Fine, but only vintage staples can be used on books from Very Fine to Near Mint. Mint books must have original staples.

PAPER/INTERIOR - Paper is off-white to cream, supple and fresh. No hint of acidity in the odor of the newsprint. Centerfold is secure. Slight interior tears are allowed.

NM-

BINDERY/PRINTING
limited number of
minor defects

COVER INKS/GLOSS
bright with slightest
dimming of reflectivity

COVER WEAR
flat, no wear, generally centered,
secure

COVER CREASES
1/16-1/8" bend with no color
break allowed

SOILING, STAINING
none allowed except for
slight foxing

DATES/STAMPS
small, inconspicuous
dates/initials allowed

SPINE ROLL
tight and flat, no roll

SPINE SPLIT
none allowed

STAPLES
some discoloration

STAPLE TEARS
none allowed

RUST MIGRATION
none allowed

STRESS LINES
almost no lines

CORNERS
ever-so-slight blunting, no creases

CENTERFOLD
secure

INTERIOR TEARS
slight tears allowed

PAPER QUALITY/COLOR
off-white to cream,
supple and fresh

ACID ODOR
none allowed

MISSING PIECES
none allowed

AMATEUR REPAIRS
none allowed

COUPON CUT
none allowed

READABILITY
preserved

Weird Comics #1, April 1940. © Fox Features Syndicate.
Obvious defects: Minor corner abrasion and small spine tear.
Hidden defects: None.
OWL: 8.

Abraded
corner

Minor
chipping

Small spine
tear

1/8" bend
(no color
break)

Blunted
corner

Shield-Wizard Comics #1, Summer 1940. © Archie Publications.
Obvious defects: Oxidation shadow on cover's right edge.
Hidden defects: None.
OWL: 8.

Corner
chip

NM-

Oxidation
shadow

Oxidation
shadow

Staple
discoloration

Spine
stress
line

Edge
chip

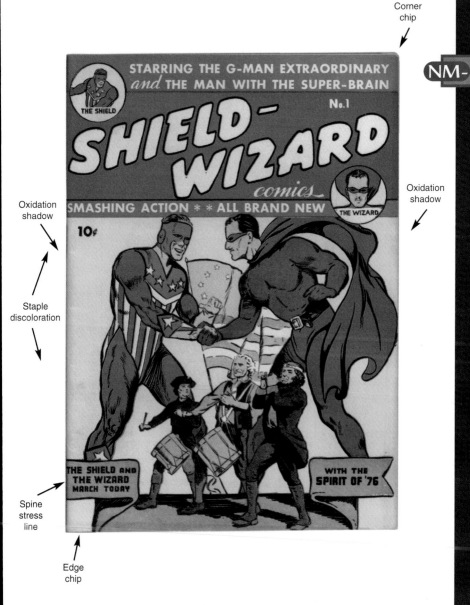

Superboy #1, March-April 1949. © DC.
Obvious defects: Slightly miswrapped cover.
Hidden defects: Ink smudges.
OWL: **8**.

NM-

1/8" bend
(no color break)

Abraded
corner

Slight
cover
color
dimming

Oxidation
shadow

Ink
smudges

Miswrapped
cover

Mad #1, Oct.-Nov. 1952. © EC
Obvious defects: Slightly stressed edges.
Hidden defects: Slight interior tears.
OWL: 7.

Stressed
edge

NM-

Staple
stress
line

Corner
chip

Edge
stress

The Incredible Hulk #1, May 1962. © Marvel.
Obvious defects: Minor spine and corner stress.
Hidden defects: None.
OWL: 7.

Corner
chip

NM−

Spine
stress

Slight
foxing

Abraded
corner

Chip

Atari Force #1, January 1984. © Atari, Inc.
Obvious defects: Blunted edges and corners.
Hidden defects: None.
OWL: 10.

Slight
blunting

Blunted
corner

NM-

Light
rubbing

Slight blunting

Subtle
corner
wrinkles

X-Factor #1, February 1986. © Marvel Characters, Inc.
Obvious defects: Miswrapped cover.
Hidden defects: Slight interior tears.
OWL: 9.

Bindery
defect

Slight
bend

NM-

Small
bumps

Over-cover

Walt Disney's Uncle Scrooge #235, July 1989. © Walt Disney Company.
Obvious defects: Blunted edge.
Hidden defects: None.
OWL: 9.

Blunted
edge

Slight staple
discoloration

Blunted
edge

Slight
bump

Slightly
impacted
corner

Gen13 #3, July 1995. © WildStorm Productions.
Obvious defects: Spine creases.
Hidden defects: None.
OWL: 10.

Blunted
corner

Edge chip

NM-

Numerous
spine
creases

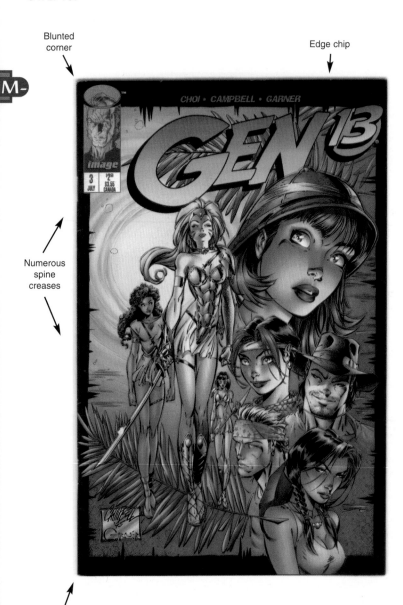

Abraded
corner

Ultimate Spider-Man #1, October 2000. © Marvel Characters, Inc.
Obvious defects: Subtle color loss near spine.
Hidden defects: Small chip in upper right corner.
OWL: 10.

Minor color loss

Minor corner chip

Minor crease around staple

Crescent crease

Color loss

NM-

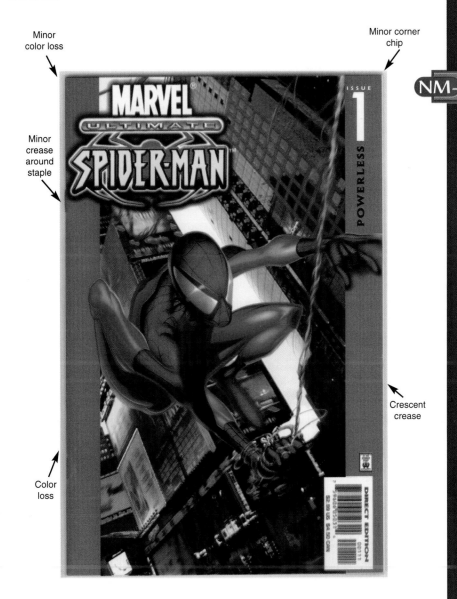

(9.0) VERY FINE/ NEAR MINT (VF/NM)

GRADE DESCRIPTION:
Nearly perfect with outstanding eye appeal. The overall look is "as if it was just purchased from the newsstand and read a few times."

BINDERY DEFECTS · A limited number of defects are allowed.

COVER/EXTERIOR · Almost flat with almost imperceptible wear. Inks are bright with slightly diminished reflectivity. An 1/8" bend is allowed if color is not broken. Corners are cut square and sharp with ever-so-slight blunting permitted but no creases. Several lightly penciled, stamped or inked arrival dates are acceptable. No obvious soiling, staining or other discoloration, except for very minor foxing.

SPINE · Tight and flat. No spine roll or split allowed.

STAPLES · Staples may show some discoloration. Only the slightest staple tears are allowed. A very minor accumulation of stress lines may be present if they are nearly imperceptible. No rust migration. In rare cases, a comic was not stapled at the bindery and therefore has a missing staple; this is not considered a defect. Any staple can be replaced on books up to Fine, but only vintage staples can be used on books from Very Fine to Near Mint. Mint books must have original staples.

PAPER/INTERIOR · Paper is off-white to cream and supple. No hint of acidity in the odor of the newsprint. Centerfold is secure. Very minor interior tears may be present.

Collectors should thoroughly examine any such book for restoration, particularly in the case of pre-1965 books. This is a crucial grade that is often misused when a book actually falls in either Very Fine or Near Mint.

BINDERY/PRINTING

limited number of defects

COVER INKS/GLOSS

bright with slightly
diminished reflectivity

COVER WEAR

almost flat, imperceptible wear

COVER CREASES

1/8" bend with no
color break allowed

SOILING, STAINING

very minor foxing

DATES/STAMPS

several dates, stamps,
and/or initials allowed

VF/NM

SPINE ROLL

tight and flat, no roll

SPINE SPLIT

none allowed

STAPLES

some discoloration
allowed

STAPLE TEARS

only the slightest
tears allowed

RUST MIGRATION

none allowed

STRESS LINES

very minor accumulation of
nearly imperceptible lines

CORNERS

no creases

CENTERFOLD

secure

INTERIOR TEARS

very minor tears allowed

PAPER QUALITY/COLOR

off-white/cream, supple

ACID ODOR

none allowed

MISSING PIECES

none allowed

AMATEUR REPAIRS

none allowed

COUPON CUT

none allowed

READABILITY

preserved

Pep Comics #1, January 1940. © Archie Publications.
Obvious defects: Slight wear on edges and spine.
Hidden defects: None.
OWL: 8.

Minor edge wear

Blunted corner

VF/NM

Very slight
spine wear
and a few
stress lines

Staple
discoloration

Light dust shadow

Very slight
rounded corner

Young Allies Comics #1, Summer 1941. © Marvel Characters, Inc.
Obvious defects: Slight corner wear.
Hidden defects: None.
OWL: 8.

Very slight
edge rub

Pencil
mark

Very slight
staple
stress

Staple
discoloration

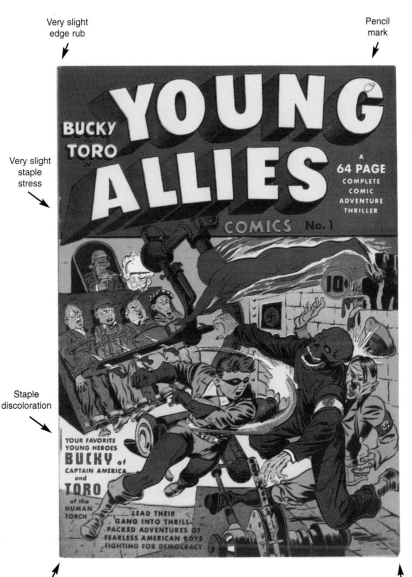

Very slight
corner rub

Blunted
corner

Showcase #4, Sept.-Oct. 1956. © DC Comics.
Obvious defects: Abraded corners.
Hidden defects: None.
OWL: **8**.

Abraded
corner

Very slight
discoloration

Slight
staple
tear

Slight
spine
stress
lines

Abraded
corner

Showcase #9, July-Aug. 1957. © DC Comics.
Obvious defects: Stressed corners.
Hidden defects: None.
OWL: 8.

Minor
corner
abrasion

Stressed
edge

Minor
discoloration

Spine
stress

Black ink
writing

VF/NM

Blunted
corner

Blunted
edge

Amazing Spider-Man #1, March 1963. © Marvel Characters, Inc.
Obvious defects: Minor corner abrasion and small spine creases.
Hidden defects: None.
OWL: 8.

Minor corner abrasion

Minor wear

VF/NM

Slight cover color dimming

Staple not centered

Small spine creases

Minor wear

Minor wear

Teen Titans #1, Jan.-Feb. 1966. © DC Comics.
Obvious defects: "#1" written in blue ink on cover.
Hidden defects: Small edge stress marks.
OWL: 9.

Minor corner
blunting

VF/NM

Blue ink
writing

Small
spine
creases

Chip

Slight
tear

Edge
stress

Arrgh! #1, December 1974. © Marvel Characters, Inc.
Obvious defects: Over-cover.
Hidden defects: None.
OWL: 9.

Small tear

Minor chipping

Corner crease

VF/NM

Minor corner

Over-cover extends 1/8"

The Destructor #4, August 1975. © Seaboard Publications.
Obvious defects: None.
Hidden defects: Minor interior tears.
OWL: 9.

Slight travelled
cover

Slight
blunting

VF/NM

Stress
line

Slight
edge wear

3/32"
spine
bend

Color flecks

Marvel Team-Up #54, February 1977. © Marvel Characters, Inc.
Obvious defects: Over-cover.
Hidden defects: None.
OWL: 8.

Corner
chip out

Small stains

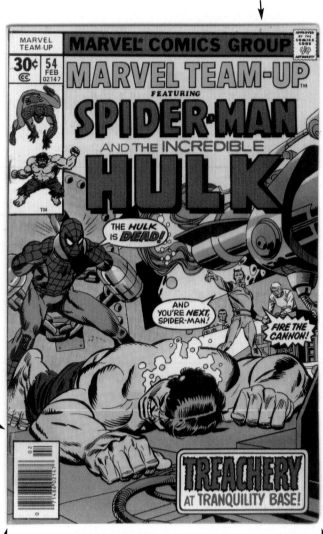

Color
fleck

Abraded
corner

Over-cover
by 1/8"

Daredevil #156, January 1979. © Marvel Characters, Inc.
Obvious defects: None.
Hidden defects: None.
OWL: 9.

Minor color
fade

1/8" corner
bend

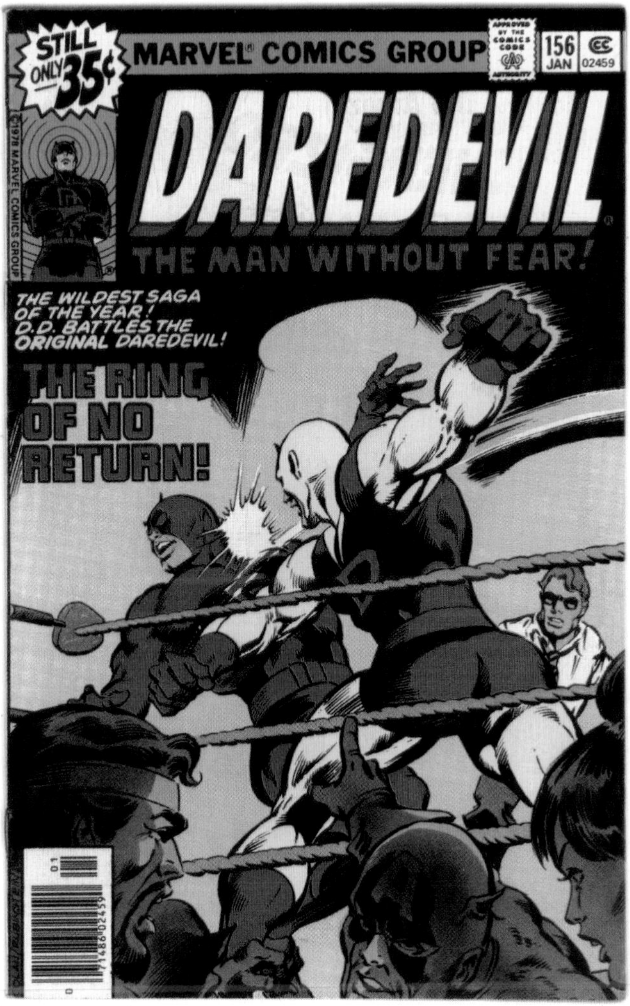

VF/NM

Small
tear at
staple

Minor
corner
abrasion

Small
corner
fold

(8.0) VERY FINE (VF)

GRADE DESCRIPTION:
An excellent copy with outstanding eye appeal. Sharp, bright and clean with supple pages. A comic book in this grade has the appearance of having been carefully handled.

BINDERY DEFECTS - A limited accumulation of minor defects is allowed.

VF

COVER/EXTERIOR - Relatively flat with minimal surface wear beginning to show, possibly including some minute wear at corners. Inks are generally bright with moderate to high reflectivity. An unnoticeable 1/4" crease is acceptable if color is not broken. Stamped or inked arrival dates may be present. No obvious soiling, staining or other discoloration, except for minor foxing.

SPINE - Almost completely flat with a possible minor color break.

STAPLES - Staples may show some discoloration. Very slight staple tears and a few almost insignificant stress lines may be present. No rust migration. In rare cases, a comic was not stapled at the bindery and therefore has a missing staple; this is not considered a defect. Any staple can be replaced on books up to Fine, but only vintage staples can be used on books from Very Fine to Near Mint. Mint books must have original staples.

PAPER/INTERIOR - Paper is cream to tan and supple. No hint of acidity in the odor of the newsprint. Centerfold is mostly secure. Minor interior tears at the margin may be present.

BINDERY/PRINTING

limited accumulation of minor defects

COVER INKS/GLOSS

generally bright with moderate to high reflectivity

COVER WEAR

relatively flat with minimal wear

COVER CREASES

unnoticeable 1/4" bend with no color break allowed

SOILING, STAINING

minor foxing

DATES/STAMPS

dates, initials, and store stamps allowed

SPINE ROLL

almost completely flat

SPINE SPLIT

minor color break allowed

VF

STAPLES

some discoloration allowed

STAPLE TEARS

very slight tears allowed

RUST MIGRATION

none allowed

STRESS LINES

a few almost insignificant lines allowed

CORNERS

minute wear allowed

CENTERFOLD

mostly secure

INTERIOR TEARS

minor tears in margin allowed

PAPER QUALITY/COLOR

cream/tan, supple

ACID ODOR

none allowed

MISSING PIECES

none allowed

AMATEUR REPAIRS

none allowed

COUPON CUT

none allowed

READABILITY

preserved

Top-Notch Comics #1, March 1939. © MLJ Magazines.
Edgar Church (Mile High) pedigree copy.
Obvious defects: Light soiling on edge. Minor spine stress.
Hidden defects: None.
OWL: 10.

VF

Grease pencil marks

Light soiling

Minor stress

Color fleck

Minor spine stress

Minute wear on corner

Captain Marvel Adventures #4, October 1941. © Fawcett Publications.
Obvious defects: Small chips on edge. Abraded corners.
Hidden defects: None.
OWL: 7.

Corner
tear

Small
edge
chips

Slight
browning
on edge

Very
minor
chip

Abraded
corner

Small chips

Superman #2, Fall 1939. © DC Comics.
Obvious defects: Chipping on edges and corners. Oxidation shadow on cover bottom.
Hidden defects: None.
OWL: 8.

Corner
chips

Soiling
line

Edge
chip

VF

Light
soiling

Slight
staple
stress

Edge
chip

Corner
chip

Oxidation
shadow

Blunted
corner

Wonder Woman #1, Summer 1942. © DC Comics.
Obvious defects: Minor creases. Abraded corner. Small spots on title logo.
Hidden defects: None.
OWL: 9.

Minor
creases

Small
spots

Corner
creases

Very
small
staple
tears

Minor
browning
on edge

VF

Staple
discoloration

Abraded
corner

Blunted
corner

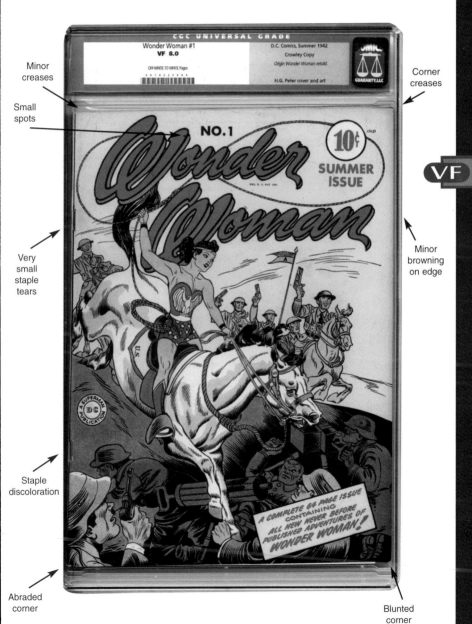

All Select Comics #1, Fall 1943. © Marvel Characters, Inc.
Obvious defects: Chipping on edges and corners.
Hidden defects: None.
OWL: 8.

Corner chip

Edge chips

Slight corner crease

VF

Spine stress

Abraded corner

Chipping

Superman-Tim, May 1946. © DC Comics.
Obvious defects: Minor chipping. Color loss from handling or printer defects.
Hidden defects: None.
OWL: 9.

Corner chip

Stress line

Color loss

Stress line

Spine chips

VF

Color chip

Color loss

SEE PAGES 8 AND 9

Official Superman-Tim Store

Abraded corner

Corner chip

Jughead as Captain Hero #1, October 1966. © Archie Publications.
Obvious defects: Slight browning on right edge of cover.
Hidden defects: None.
OWL: 9.

Slight
crease

Browning
along
edge

VF

Rubbing

Color
loss

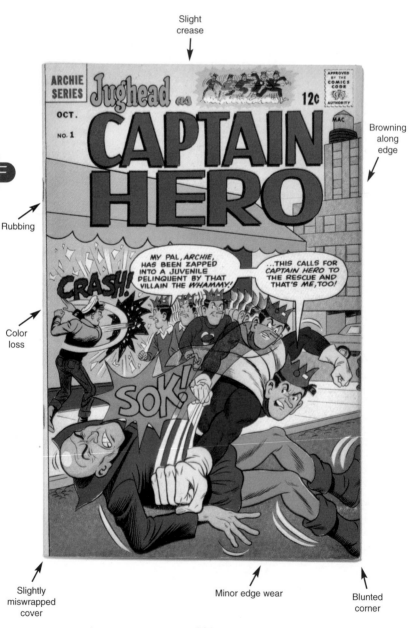

Slightly
miswrapped
cover

Minor edge wear

Blunted
corner

Teen Titans #14, March-April 1968. © DC Comics.
Obvious defects: Small spine and corner creases.
Hidden defects: None.
OWL: 10.

Corner
creases

Corner
creases

Edge
creases

VF

Spine
creases

Minor
abraded
corner

Color fleck
in corner

Silver Surfer #1, August 1968. © Marvel Characters, Inc.
Obvious defects: None.
Hidden defects: Minor soiling and fingerprints on title letters.
OWL: 9.

Minor corner
abrasion

Visible fingerprints and
faint ink residue on white
title letters

VF

Spine
stress
lines

Minor
pin
hole

Corner
chip

Edge stress

The Avengers #187, September 1979. © Marvel Characters, Inc.
Obvious defects: Color chips near edges.
Hidden defects: None.
OWL: 9.

Minor
foxing

Color
chips

Light
crease

VF

Minor
color
break

Browning
on edge

Slight corner bend
(no color break)

Funnies On Parade, 1933. © Eastern Color.
Obvious defects: Light soiling over most of the cover. Some corner wear visible.
Hidden defects: Light tan pages.
OWL: 6.

Missing chip

Missing chip

Abraded corner

VF

Slight discoloration

Abraded corner

Chipped edge

Corner crease

Iron Man #1, May 1968. © Marvel Characters, Inc.
Obvious defects: Top of back cover not trimmed to match the rest of the comic.
Hidden defects: Some interior pages have corner tears.
OWL: 9.

Minor
abraded
corner

High cover gloss.
Flat cover

Minor creases

Minor
corner
creases

VF

Minor
spine
stress

Minor
spine
stress

Abraded
corner

Minor
color
flecks

(7.0) **FINE/VERY FINE** (F/VF)

GRADE DESCRIPTION:
An above-average copy that shows minor wear but is still relatively flat and clean with outstanding eye appeal. A comic book in this grade appears to have been read a few times and has been handled with care.

BINDERY DEFECTS - A small accumulation of minor defects is allowed.

COVER/EXTERIOR - Minor wear beginning to show, possibly including minor creases. Corners may be blunted. Inks are generally bright with a moderate reduction in reflectivity. Stamped or inked arrival dates may be present. No obvious soiling, staining or other discoloration, except for minor foxing.

SPINE - The slightest roll may be present, as well as a possible moderate color break.

STAPLES - Staples may show some discoloration. Slight staple tears and a small accumulation of light stress lines may be present. Slight rust migration. In rare cases, a comic was not stapled at the bindery and therefore has a missing staple; this is not considered a defect. Any staple can be replaced on books up to Fine, but only vintage staples can be used on books from Very Fine to Near Mint. Mint books must have original staples.

PAPER/INTERIOR - Paper is cream to tan, but not brown. No hint of acidity in the odor of the newsprint. Centerfold is mostly secure. Minor interior tears at the margin may be present.

BINDERY/PRINTING
small accumulation of
minor defects

COVER INKS/GLOSS
moderate reduction in reflectivity

COVER WEAR
minimal wear, interior yellowing
or tanning allowed

COVER CREASES
minor creases allowed

SOILING, STAINING
minor foxing

DATES/STAMPS
dates, initials, and
store stamps allowed

SPINE ROLL
slightest roll allowed

SPINE SPLIT
moderate color break allowed

STAPLES
some discoloration
allowed

STAPLE TEARS
slight tears
allowed

RUST MIGRATION
slight migration
allowed

F/VF

STRESS LINES
small accumulation of
light lines

CORNERS
may be blunted

CENTERFOLD
mostly secure

INTERIOR TEARS
minor tears in margin allowed

PAPER QUALITY/COLOR
cream/tan, not brown

ACID ODOR
none allowed

MISSING PIECES
none allowed

AMATEUR REPAIRS
none allowed

COUPON CUT
none allowed

READABILITY
preserved

Billy the Kid and Oscar #1, Winter 1945. © Fawcett Publications.
Obvious defects: Out of register cover printing.
Hidden defects: Minor soiling at bottom of cover.
OWL: 7.

Crumpled corner

Stamp

Library of Congress stamp

Stamp

Writing

F/VF

Slight rust migration on staple

Minor soiling

Weird Science #14, Sept.-Oct. 1950. © William M. Gaines.
Obvious defects: Missing chips. Minor spine roll.
Hidden defects: None.
OWL: 9.

Blunted
corner

Corner
chip

Slight
roll

Spine
creases

Slight
foxing

F/VF

Slight
corner
stress

Minor
foxing

Blunted
corner

Weird Science-Fantasy Annual 1953. © William M. Gaines.
Obvious defects: Squrebound spine shows some wear.
Hidden defects: None.
OWL: 9.
Note: High cover gloss.

Abraded corner

Reading crease

High reflectivity

Corner creases

Spine tear

F/VF

Tear

Corner wear

Crease

Chip

Crease

Crease

Tales From the Crypt #41, May 1954. © William M. Gaines.
Obvious defects: Spine creases and minor browning on inside cover only.
Hidden defects: Corner chipping on numerous interior pages.
OWL: 8.
Note: High cover gloss. Copy is flat.

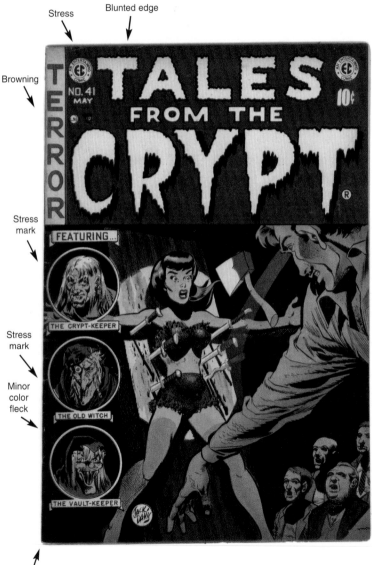

My Little Margie #1, August 1956. © Charlton Comics Group.
Mile High pedigree copy.
Obvious defects: Bindery defect miswrapped cover.
Hidden defects: Staple holes through all interior pages.
OWL: 8.

F/VF

Miswrapped
cover

Spine
chip

Staple
holes
running
through
entire
comic

Reading
crease

Minor
abraded
corner

My Little Margie #1
(Back cover)

Miswrapped
cover

F/VF

Mild
soiling

Spine
creases

Ben Bowie and his Mountain Men #11, May-July 1957. © Western Publishing Co.
Pennsylvania pedigree copy shown.
Obvious defects: Arrival date written on title letters.
Hidden defects: Minor spine creases.
OWL: 10.

Minor edge
stress

Color flecking
on edge

Corner
stress

Writing

F/VF

Small
spine
creases

Two
pin
holes

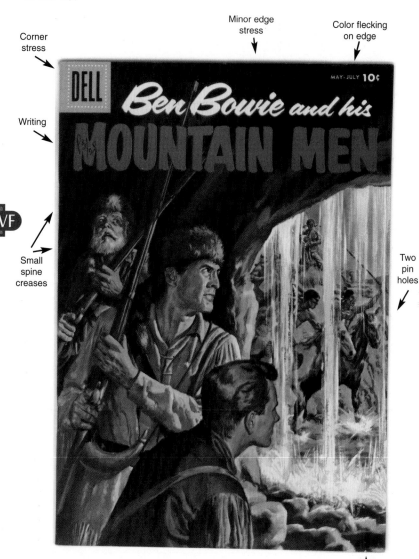

Edge
chip

Amazing Fantasy #15, August 1962. © Marvel Characters, Inc.
Obvious defects: Small creases along the entire spine. Corner chip and abrasion.
Hidden defects: None.
OWL: 8.

Edge crease

Corner chip

Minor staple stress

Small spine creases

Staple stress

Abraded corner

F/VF

Edge wear

Minor tears

Justice League of America #92, September 1971. © DC Comics.
Obvious defects: Mild spine stress.
Hidden defects: Mild soiling on back cover along spine.
OWL: 9.

Distributor color coding

Spine stress

Spine stress

F/VF

Small accumulation
of light lines

Spawn #1, May 1992. © Todd McFarlane.
Obvious defects: Color scrapes near spine. Abraded corners.
Hidden defects: None.
OWL: 10.

Abraded
corner

Slight
crease

Edge
chip

Color
scrapes

F/VF

Spine
tear

Corner
bend

Slight color flecking
on edge

Corner
chip

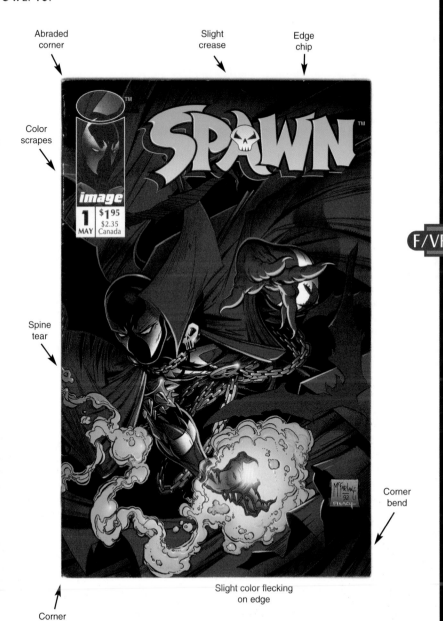

(6.0) FINE (FN)

GRADE DESCRIPTION:
An above-average copy that shows minor wear but is still relatively flat and clean with no significant creasing or other serious defects. Eye appeal is somewhat reduced because of slight surface wear and the accumulation of small defects, especially on the spine and edges. A FINE condition comic book appears to have been read a few times and has been handled with moderate care.

BINDERY DEFECTS - Some accumulation of minor defects is allowed.

COVER/EXTERIOR - Minor wear apparent, with minor to moderate creases. Inks show a significant reduction in reflectivity. Blunted corners are more common, as is minor staining, soiling, discoloration, and/or foxing. Stamped or inked arrival dates may be present.

SPINE - A minor spine roll is allowed. There can also be a 1/4" spine split or severe color break.

STAPLES - Staples may show minor discoloration. Minor staple tears and a few slight stress lines may be present, as well as minor rust migration. In rare cases, a comic was not stapled at the bindery and therefore has a missing staple; this is not considered a defect. Any staple can be replaced on books up to Fine, but only vintage staples can be used on books from Very Fine to Near Mint. Mint books must have original staples.

PAPER/INTERIOR - Paper is tan to brown and fairly supple with no signs of brittleness. No hint of acidity in the odor of the newsprint. Minor interior tears at the margin may be present. Centerfold may be loose but not detached.

FINE has historically been the most difficult grade to identify. It is the highest grade which allows a wide range of defects to occur.

BINDERY/PRINTING
some accumulation of minor defects

COVER INKS/GLOSS
significant reduction in reflectivity

COVER WEAR
minor wear

COVER CREASES
minor to moderate creases

SOILING, STAINING
minor discoloration, staining, and/or foxing

DATES/STAMPS
dates/initials/stamps allowed

SPINE ROLL
minor roll allowed

SPINE SPLIT
up to 1/4" split or severe color break allowed

STAPLES
minor discoloration allowed

STAPLE TEARS
minor tears allowed

RUST MIGRATION
minor migration allowed

FN

STRESS LINES
few slight lines

CORNERS
blunting more common

CENTERFOLD
loose, not detached

INTERIOR TEARS
minor tears in margin

PAPER QUALITY/COLOR
tan/brown, supple, not brittle

ACID ODOR
none allowed

MISSING PIECES
none allowed

AMATEUR REPAIRS
none allowed

COUPON CUT
none allowed

READABILITY
preserved

Captain America Comics #1, March 1941. © Marvel Characters, Inc.
Obvious defects: Spine shows some wear. Color flecks near spine.
Hidden defects: None.
OWL: 8.

Color
flecks

Missing
chip

Browning
on edge

Worn
spine

Erased
letters

FN

Light
color
loss

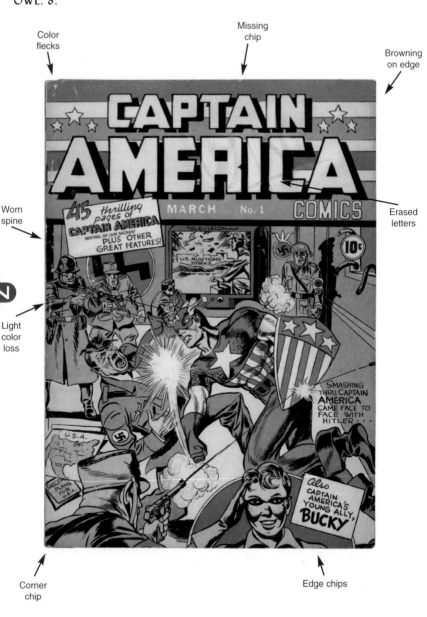

Corner
chip

Edge chips

Sub-Mariner Comics #1, Spring 1941. © Marvel Characters, Inc.
Obvious defects: Slight corner wear.
Hidden defects: None.
OWL: 7.

Abraded
corner

Slight
browning

Discolored
staple

Reduction
in
reflectivity

Minor
rubbing

Staple rust
migration

Corner
chip

Minor
wear

Adventures of the Big Boy #100. © Robert C. Wian Enterprises, Inc.
Obvious defects: Rectangular tape residue on title logo. Slight water damage and slight crease on back cover.
Hidden defects: The paper cover has subtle stains, including slight soiling on back cover.
OWL: 8.

Tape residue

Minor soiling

Close-up of
tape residue

Adventures of the Big Boy #100 (back cover)

Slight
soiling

Small
tear

Green Lantern #1, Fall 1941. © DC Comics.
Obvious defects: Chipped edge. Slightly miswrapped cover.
Hidden defects: None.
OWL: 8.

Corner
wear

Blunted
corner

Pencil
mark

Foxing

Spine
tear

Chipped
edge

Miswrapped
cover

Rounded
corner

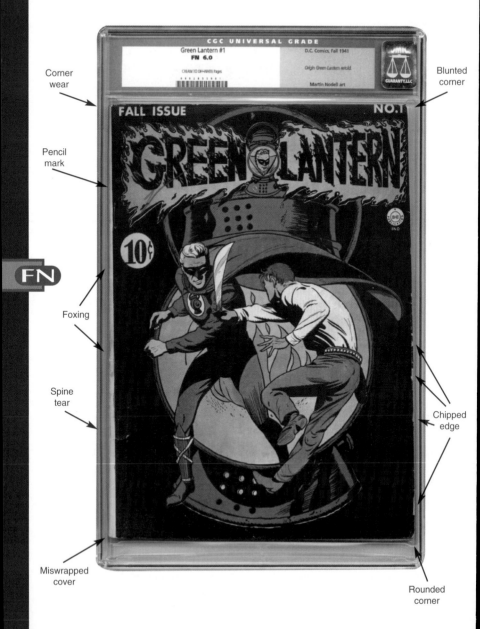

Yogi Bear Visits the U.N. ·*Four Color* #1349, 1961. © Hanna-Barbera.
Obvious defects: Cover whites have browned especially along the spine.
Hidden defects: Minor spine creases.
OWL: 8.

Corner
chip out

Browning

Corner
chip

Browning
along
spine

FN

Small
spine tear

Crease

Corner
chip

Underdog #1, July 1970. © Charlton Press.
Obvious defects: Oxidation shadow on top of cover.
Hidden defects: Fanned pages.
OWL: 8.

Slight
water mark

Oxidation
shadow

Oxidation
shadows

Moderate
crease

Small
cover
indentation

FN

1/4"
spine

Minor
corner
chip

Significant reduction
in reflectivity

Giant-Size Conan the Barbarian #1, September 1974. © Marvel Characters, Inc.
Obvious defects: Book shape is skewed, cover is miswrapped.
Hidden defects: None.
OWL: 10.

Book trimming defect at
incorrect angle

FN

Slight
edge
stress

Corner angle is
off by this much

Blunted
corner

Amazing Spider-Man Annual #21, 1987. © Marvel Characters, Inc.
Obvious defects: Off center top staple. Water damage on bottom of cover.
Hidden defects: Light soiling.
OWL: **8**.

Small corner creases

Off-centered

Minor crease

Off center staple

Stress line

FN

Small tear

Light corner crease

Minor soiling

Crease

Slight browning

Water damage

All-American Comics #16, July 1940. © DC Comics.
Obvious defects: Some chipping on edges.
Hidden defects: None.
OWL: 7.

Corner chip

Pencil marks

Bundling ridge

Rounded corner

Light soiling

Crease

FN

Foxing

Blunted corner

Abraded edge

Small crease

Small chips

The Human Torch #6, Winter 1941. © Marvel Characters, Inc.
Obvious defects: Browning on spine. Corners show wear.
Hidden defects: Slight spine roll.
OWL: 7.

Amazing Spider-Man #109, June 1972. © Marvel Characters Inc.
Obvious defects: Several spine stress lines. Significant reduction of reflectivity
on back cover.
Hidden defects: Minor stains inside back cover.
OWL: 9.

Abraded corner

Creases

Moderate corner creases on back cover

Several spine stress lines

Silver ink autograph

Spine crease

Moderate crease on bottom back cover

Corner crease

(5.0) VERY GOOD/FINE (VG/FN)

GRADE DESCRIPTION:
An above-average but well-used comic book. A comic in this grade shows some moderate wear; eye appeal is somewhat reduced because of the accumulation of defects. Still a desirable copy that has been handled with some care.

BINDERY DEFECTS · An accumulation of defects is allowed.

COVER/EXTERIOR · Minor to moderate wear apparent, with minor to moderate creases and/or dimples. Inks have moderate to low reflectivity. Blunted corners are increasingly common, as is minor to moderate staining, discoloration, and/or foxing. Stamped or inked arrival dates may be present.

SPINE · A minor to moderate spine roll is allowed. A spine split of up to 1/2" may be present.

STAPLES · Staples may show minor discoloration. Minor staple tears and minor stress lines may also be present, as well as minor rust migration. In rare cases, a comic was not stapled at the bindery and therefore has a missing staple; this is not considered a defect. Any staple can be replaced on books up to Fine, but only vintage staples can be used on books from Very Fine to Near Mint. Mint books must have original staples.

PAPER/INTERIOR · Paper is tan to brown with no signs of brittleness. May have the beginning of an acidic odor. Centerfold may be loose but not detached. Minor interior tears may also be present.

BINDERY/PRINTING
accumulation of defects

COVER INKS/GLOSS
moderate to low reflectivity

COVER WEAR
minor to moderate wear

COVER CREASES
minor to moderate
creases and dimples

SOILING, STAINING
minor to moderate discoloration,
staining, and/or foxing

DATES/STAMPS
dates/initials/stamps allowed

SPINE ROLL
minor to moderate roll

SPINE SPLIT
up to 1/2" split

STAPLES
minor discoloration

STAPLE TEARS
minor tears

RUST MIGRATION
minor migration

STRESS LINES
minor lines

CORNERS
blunting increasingly common

VG/FN

CENTERFOLD
loose, not detached

INTERIOR TEARS
minor tears

PAPER QUALITY/COLOR
tan/brown to brown,
not brittle

ACID ODOR
may have beginning of odor

MISSING PIECES
none allowed

AMATEUR REPAIRS
none allowed

COUPON CUT
none allowed

READABILITY
preserved

Adventure Comics #40, July 1939. © DC Comics.
Obvious defects: Rat chew and light soiling.
Hidden defects: None.
OWL: 8.

Corner
chip

Light
foxing

Rat
chew

Rumpled
cover

VG/FN

Staple
stress

Abraded
corner

Star Spangled Comics #1, October 1941. © DC Comics.
Obvious defects: Browning on edges. Color chips missing from corners.
Hidden defects: None.
OWL: 6.

Color chip

Color chip

Color flecks

Spine chips

Spine tear

Browning

Browning

1/2" spine split

Browning

Blunted corner

VG/FN

Green Hornet Comics #29, March 1946. © The Green Hornet Inc.
Obvious defects: Poorly trimmed interior pages.
Hidden defects: None.
OWL: 7.

Torn corner

Poorly trimmed interior pages

Rust migration from staple

Minor tear

VG/FN

1" tear

Oxidation shadow

Book has a slight odor

Green Hornet Comics #29
(Interior pages)

VG/FN

The Lone Ranger #6, Nov.-Dec. 1948. © Lone Ranger Inc.
Obvious defects: Small creases on spine. Color flecking on edge.
Hidden defects: Some interior pages have perforations on edge from printing.
OWL: 9.

Worn edge

Color scrape

Chip

Numerous
small
spine
creases

VG/FN

Color
flecking

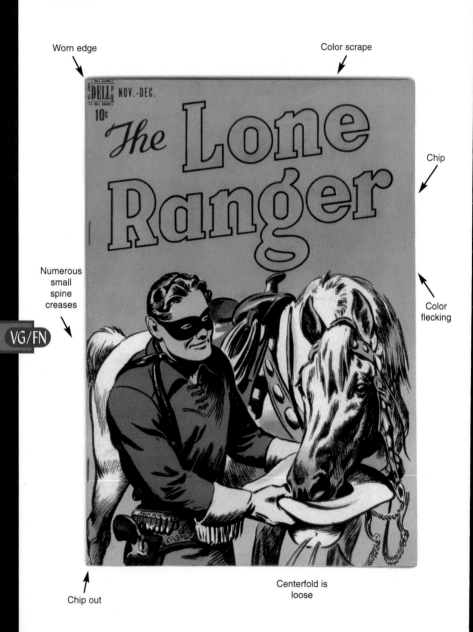

Chip out

Centerfold is
loose

Walt Disney's Comics and Stories #131, August 1951. © Walt Disney Company.
Obvious defects: Spine creases.
Hidden defects: Top of book not trimmed squarely.
OWL: 9.

Corner
tear

Slightly
worn corner

Spine
wrinkling

Cover
rumpled

Staple
tear

VG/FN

Spine
creases

Cover
edge
wear

Staple
tear

Spine
stress

Color
flecks

Creases

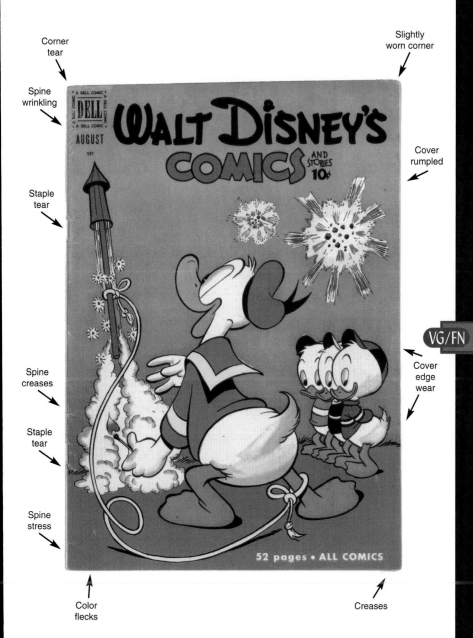

Kid Colt Outlaw #72, May 1957. © Marvel Characters, Inc.
Circle 8 pedigree copy. Copy has high cover gloss.
Obvious defects: Frayed corners and spine.
Hidden defects: None.
OWL: 9.

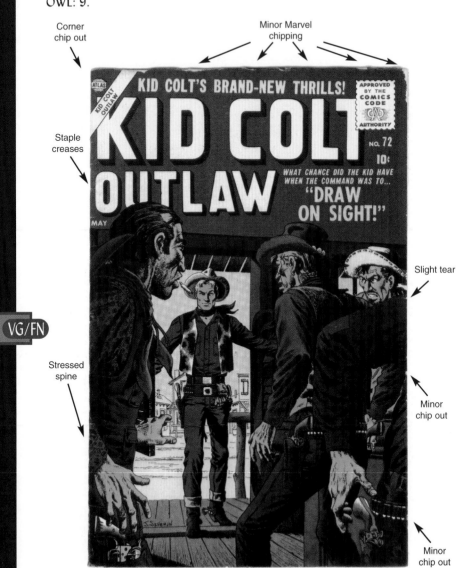

Corner chip out

Minor Marvel chipping

Staple creases

Slight tear

VG/FN

Stressed spine

Minor chip out

Minor chip out

Abraded corner

Our Army at War #138, January 1964. © DC Comics.
Obvious defects: Corner creases.
Hidden defects: Loose upper staple.
OWL: 8.

Astro Boy #1, August 1965. © NBC, Inc.
Obvious defects: Tape residue lines on lower 2" of cover. Staining on edge.
Hidden defects: None.
OWL: 9.

Abraded
corner

Corner
stains

Edge
stains

VG/FN

Edge
browning

Tape residue
running across book

Shazam! #1, February 1973. © DC Comics.
Obvious defects: Light soiling on front and back covers.
Hidden defects: None.
OWL: 9.

1/2"
spine
split

1/8"
corner
crease

Staple
tear

Small
spine
creases

Edge
tear

VG/FN

Staple
stress
lines

Crease

(4.0) VERY GOOD (VG)

GRADE DESCRIPTION:
The average used comic book. A comic in this grade shows some significant moderate wear, but still has not accumulated enough total defects to reduce eye appeal to the point that it is not a desirable copy.

COVER/EXTERIOR - Cover shows moderate to significant wear, and may be loose but not completely detached. Cover reflectivity is low. Can have moderate creases or dimples. Corners may be blunted. Store stamps, name stamps, arrival dates, initials, etc. have no effect on this grade. Some discoloration, fading, foxing, and even minor soiling is allowed. As much as a 1/4" triangle can be missing out of the corner or edge; a missing 1/8" square is also acceptable. Only minor unobtrusive tape and other amateur repair allowed on otherwise high grade copies.

SPINE - Moderate roll may be present and/or a 1" spine split.

STAPLES - Staples may be discolored. Minor to moderate staple tears and stress lines may be present, as well as some rust migration.

PAPER/INTERIOR - Paper is brown but not brittle. A minor acidic odor can be detectable. Minor to moderate interior tears may be present. Centerfold may be loose or detached at one staple.

Comics in this condition are still desirable and collectable. The best known copies of some pre-1965 books are in VG condition.

There are significant differences between this grade and GOOD; over-grading sometimes occurs.

BINDERY/PRINTING
do not affect grade

COVER INKS/GLOSS
low reflectivity

COVER WEAR
moderate to significant wear,
may be loose

COVER CREASES
moderate creases or dimples

SOILING, STAINING
some discoloration, fading,
foxing, even minor soiling

DATES/STAMPS
do not affect grade

SPINE ROLL
moderate roll

SPINE SPLIT
up to 1" split

STAPLES
discolored

STAPLE TEARS
minor to moderate
tears

RUST MIGRATION
some migration

STRESS LINES
minor to moderate lines

CORNERS
blunted corners

CENTERFOLD
loose or detached at one staple

INTERIOR TEARS
minor to moderate tears

VG

PAPER QUALITY/COLOR
brown, not brittle

ACID ODOR
minor odor

MISSING PIECES
1/4" triangle, 1/8" square

AMATEUR REPAIRS
minor repairs on otherwise
high grade

COUPON CUT
none allowed

READABILITY
preserved

Marvel Mystery Comics #19, May 1941. © Marvel Characters, Inc.
Obvious defects: Spine is worn and split on ends.
Hidden defects: None.
OWL: 5.

Reading crease

Color flecking

Split spine

Chip out

Spine tears

Color flecking

Staple not centered

Spine stress lines

VG

Rust migration

Split spine

Small tear

Rounded corner

Sub-Mariner Comics #4, Winter 1942. © Marvel Characters, Inc.
Obvious defects: Abraded corners. Oxidation shadows.
Hidden defects: Interior pages brown at edges.
OWL: 5.

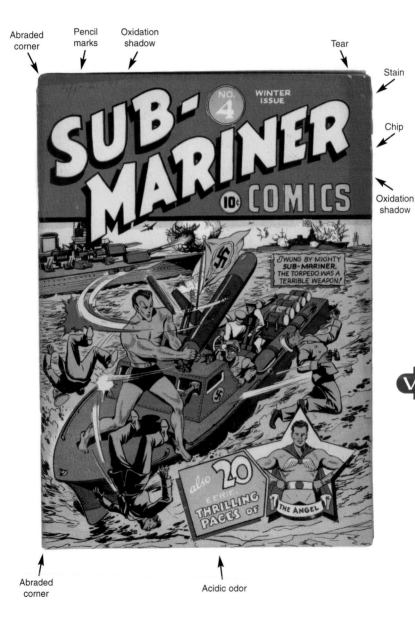

Abraded corner

Pencil marks

Oxidation shadow

Tear

Stain

Chip

Oxidation shadow

Abraded corner

Acidic odor

VG

Strange Adventures #1, Aug.-Sept. 1950. © DC Comics.
Obvious defects: Numerous chips on cover edges.
Hidden defects: Color flecks in the cover's starry sky.
OWL: 6.

Roy Rogers Comics #37, January 1951. © The ROHR Co.
Obvious defects: Numerous color flecks and creases near spine. Wrinkle through the center of the cover.
Hidden defects: None.
OWL: 8.
Note: Double cover.

Adventure Comics #59, February 1940. © DC Comics.
Obvious defects: Browning stains on cover edges.
Hidden defects: Brown interior pages.
OWL: 5.

Rounded corner

Loss of reflectivity

Writing on cover

Brown staining

Brown staining

Abraded spine

Edge wear

VG

Spine wear

1" spine tear

Minor fraying

Crease

Corner chip

All Star Comics #1, Summer 1940. © DC Comics.
Obvious defects: Spine is worn. Store stamp.
Hidden defects: Mold on interior pages.
OWL: 5.

Corner
chip out

Chip missing

Rounded
corner

Mold
stain

Abraded
spine

Store
stamp

Spine
tear

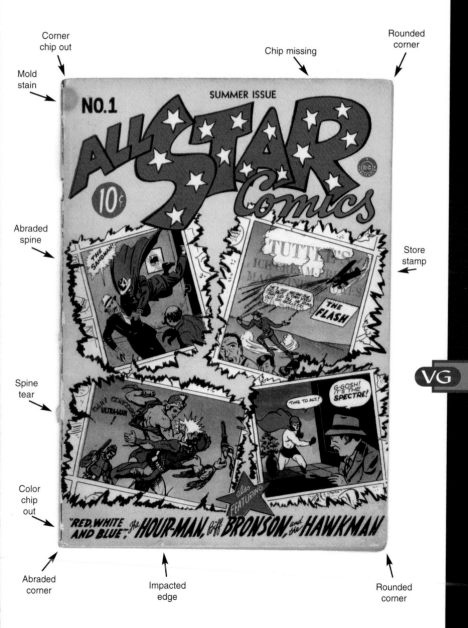

VG

Color
chip
out

Abraded
corner

Impacted
edge

Rounded
corner

Master Comics #23, February 1942. © Fawcett Publications.
Obvious defects: Worn corners.
Hidden defects: Subtle folds and creases on cover.
OWL: 8.

Corner chip out

Long, very light crease

Color flecking

Staple tear

Numerous spine creases

Minor edge

VG

Staple tear

Corner chip

Crease

Chip

Corner chip

Leading Comics #8, Fall 1943. © DC Comics.
Obvious defects: Miswrapped cover with spine roll.
Hidden defects: Blunted corner on some interior pages.
OWL: 9.

Abraded corner

Color scrape

Miswrapped cover

Pencil mark

Spine roll

Loose centerfold

Color rub

VG

Abraded corner

Color scrape

Stain

Color missing abrasion

Miswrapped cover

Out of This World #1, June 1950. © Avon Publications.
Obvious defects: Large brownish transfer stain in center of cover.
Hidden defects: Loose centerfold pages.
OWL: 7.

Abraded corner

Crease

Chip missing

Frayed edge

Rounded corner

Creases

Color loss

VG

Light long crease

Edge stain

Abraded corner

Frayed edge

Abraded corner

Intimate Confessions #1, July-Aug. 1951. © Realistic Comics.
Obvious defects: Stressed edges. Full length crease down the center of the cover.
Hidden defects: None.
OWL: 6.

Archie's Pal Jughead Comics #20, October 1953. © Archie Publications.
Obvious defects: Creases on the spine. Minor wrinkles near bottom of cover.
Hidden defects: Some interior pages have small holes or tears. Centerfold detached
at one staple.
OWL: 9.

Tear

Crease

Corner
chip

Color
fleck

Creases

VG

Tear

Creases
around
staple

Corner
chip

Tear

Crease

Creases

Fantastic Four #13, April 1963. © Marvel Characters, Inc.
Obvious defects: Marvel chipping on cover's edge.
Hidden defects: None.
OWL: 9.

Abraded corner

Edge wear

Corner chip

Marvel chipping

VG

Moderate stress lines

Abraded corner

Missing chip

Edge wear

Action Comics #1, June 1938. © DC Comics.
Obvious defects: Light soiling on most of cover.
Hidden defects: Small spine split on every page. Small amount of dried glue on spine.
OWL: 7.

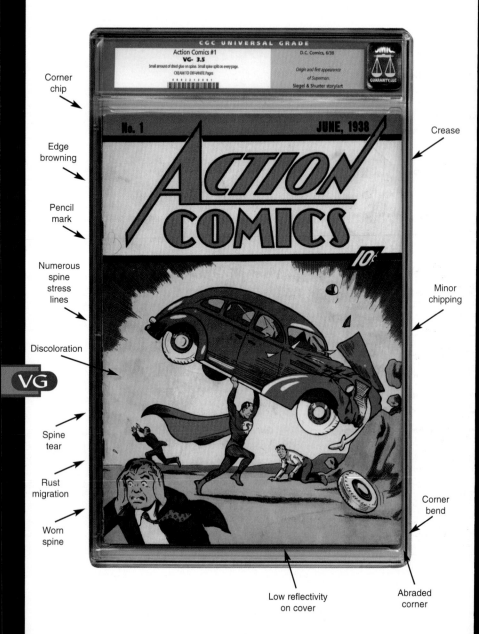

Corner chip

Edge browning

Pencil mark

Numerous spine stress lines

Discoloration

VG

Spine tear

Rust migration

Worn spine

Crease

Minor chipping

Corner bend

Abraded corner

Low reflectivity on cover

Captain America Comics #2, April 1941. © Marvel Characters, Inc.
Obvious defects: Browning on edges. Spine crease.
Hidden defects: Mild soiling.
OWL: 5.

Inaccurate trimming

Corner chipping

Edge wear

Tear

Spine crease

Cover loose

Spine stress

Chip

Browning on edge

VG

Edge chipping

Abraded corner

Mild soiling

Blunted corner

Donald Duck #147, 1947. © Walt Disney Company.
Obvious defects: Worn spine. Oxidation shadow on right edge of cover.
Hidden defects: Numerous interior pages have frayed edges.
OWL: 6.

Abraded
corner

Oxidation
shadow

Color
chip

Arrival
date in
pencil

Rusted
staple

Staple
tear

VG

Spine
creases

Name
stamp

Corner
crease

Abraded
corner

Multiple dimples
on cover

Initials written
in black ink

Corner
tear

Fantastic Four #48, March 1966. © Marvel Characters, Inc.
Obvious defects: Bindery defect of front cover wrapped 1/4" onto back.
Hidden defects: Frayed edges on some interior pages.
OWL: 9.

Abraded corner

Loose chip

Corner chip and creases

Front cover image wraps onto back by 1/4"

Numerous spine creases

VG

Chip

Reading crease

Crease with color loss

Crease

(3.0) GOOD/VERY GOOD (G/VG)

GRADE DESCRIPTION:
A used comic book showing some substantial wear. A copy in this grade has all pages and covers, although there may be small pieces missing. Still a reasonably desirable copy and completely readable.

COVER/EXTERIOR - Cover shows significant wear, and may be loose or even detached at one staple. Cover reflectivity is very low. Can have a book-length crease and/or dimples. Corners may be blunted or even rounded. Store stamps, name stamps, arrival dates, initials, etc. have no effect on this grade. Discoloration, fading, foxing, and even minor to moderate soiling is allowed. A triangle from 1/4" to 1/2" can be missing out of the corner or edge; a missing 1/8" to 1/4" square is also acceptable. Tape and other amateur repair may be present.

SPINE - Moderate roll likely. May have a spine split of anywhere from 1" to 1·1/2".

STAPLES - Staples may be rusted or replaced. Minor to moderate staple tears and moderate stress lines may be present, as well as some rust migration.

PAPER/INTERIOR - Paper is brown but not brittle. A minor to moderate acidic odor can be detectable. Centerfold may be loose or detached at one staple. Minor to moderate interior tears may be present.

BINDERY/PRINTING
do not affect grade

COVER INKS/GLOSS
very low reflectivity

COVER WEAR
significant wear, loose,
may be detached at one staple

COVER CREASES
book-length creases, dimples

SOILING, STAINING
discoloration, fading, foxing,
minor to moderate soiling

DATES/STAMPS
do not affect grade

SPINE ROLL
moderate roll likely

SPINE SPLIT
up to 1-1/2" split

STAPLES
rusted or replaced

STAPLE TEARS
minor to moderate
tears

RUST MIGRATION
some migration

STRESS LINES
moderate lines

CORNERS
blunted, may be rounded

CENTERFOLD
loose or detached at one staple

INTERIOR TEARS
minor to moderate tears

PAPER QUALITY/COLOR
brown, not brittle

ACID ODOR
minor to moderate odor

GD/VG

MISSING PIECES
1/4" to 1/2" triangle,
1/8" to 1/4" square

AMATEUR REPAIRS
may be present

COUPON CUT
none allowed

READABILITY
preserved

Nickel Comics #1, May 1940. © Fawcett Publications.
Obvious defects: Abraded spine with foxing.
Hidden defects: Foxing on interior pages.
OWL: 6.

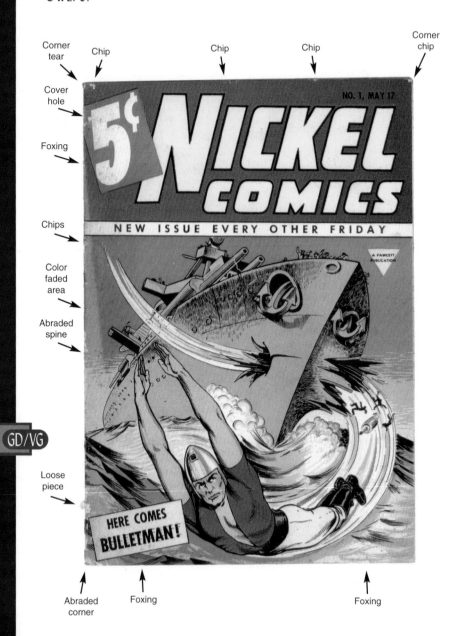

Bulletman #1, Summer 1941. © Fawcett Publications.
Obvious defects: Numerous spine chips and abrasions. Browning on edges.
Hidden defects: Loose interior pages.
OWL: 5.

Back cover spine

Abraded corner

Minor soiling

Chip

Loose and missing pieces

Spine chips

Browning on edge

Spine chips

Color flecks

Abraded spine

Mis-trimmed cover

Browning on edge

GD/VG

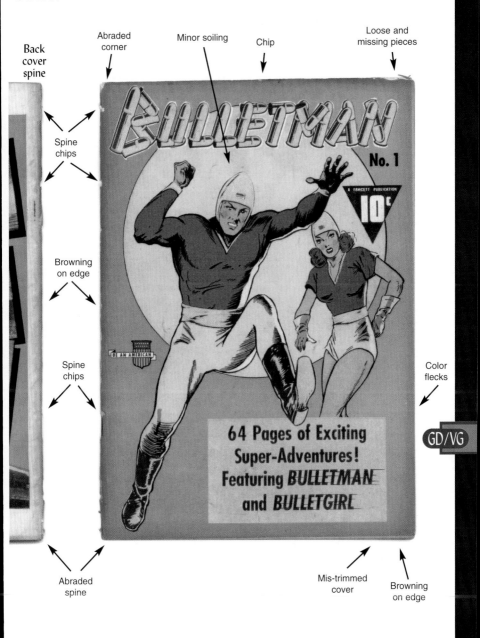

More Fun Comics #103, May-June 1945. © DC Comics.
Obvious defects: Excessive spine wear. Rusted staples.
Hidden defects: None.
OWL: **8**.

Peter Porkchops #2, Jan-Feb. 1950. © DC Comics.
Obvious defects: Spine is damaged, especially at the bottom. Numerous small tears on the right edge of the cover.
Hidden defects: Stains on the inside front cover show through to the front.
OWL: **8**.

Reading crease

Numerous tears

Corner fold

Corner chip

Staple tears

Tear

Tear

Tear

Tear

Spine tear

GD/VG

Tear

Split spine

Foxing

Foxing

Funny Folks #2, June-July 1946. © DC Comics.
Obvious defects: Numerous chips missing from cover's top edge. Cover is mis-wrapped, leaving unprinted area on right edge. Staples are rusty, with rust migration on back cover staples.
Hidden defects: None.
OWL: 7.

Abraded corner

Creases

Numerous chips missing

Missing chip

Black ink writing

Color scrape

Color scrapes

Color scrape

Small chips off cover

GD/VG

Abraded corner

Frayed edge

Mis-wrapped cover

Funny Folks #2
(Back cover)

Rusted staple

Rusted staple with rust migration

GD/VG

Amazing Adventures #1, November 1950. © Ziff-Davis Publishing Co.
Obvious defects: Numerous chips and tears near spine.
Hidden defects: None.
OWL: 8.

Rounded corner

Corner chip

Crease

Chip

Worn spine

GD/VG

Chips

Spine piece missing

Chipping all along edge

Corner chip

Eddie Stanky, Baseball Hero #1, 1951. © Fawcett Publications.
Obvious defects: Center crease on cover.
Hidden defects: Center crease on interior pages.
OWL: 9.

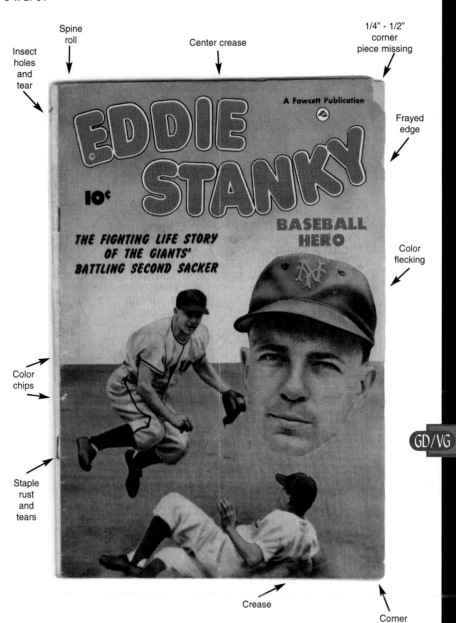

Spine roll

Center crease

1/4" - 1/2" corner piece missing

Insect holes and tear

Frayed edge

Color flecking

Color chips

Staple rust and tears

GD/VG

Crease

Corner creases

Archie's Pals 'n' Gals #1, 1952-53. © Archie Publications.
Obvious defects: Squarebound spine missing bottom half inch. Reading creases.
Hidden defects: None.
OWL: 8.

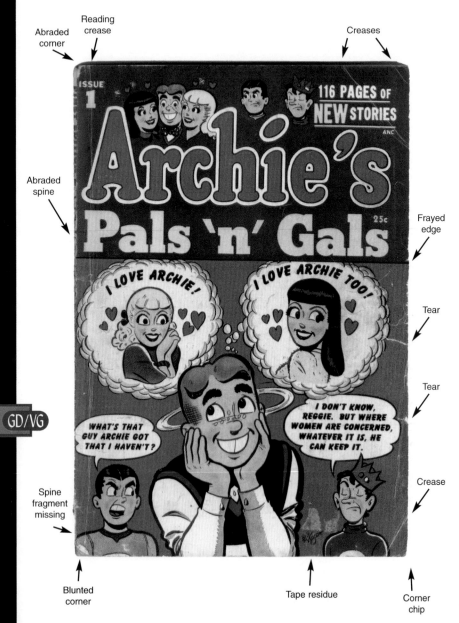

Detective Comics #283, September 1960. © DC Comics.
Obvious defects: Frayed right edge on cover.
Hidden defects: Pencil marks on interior pages.
OWL: **8**.

Corner chip out

Comic has moderate acidic odor

Loose piece still attached

Chip out

Frayed edge

Numerous spine creases

GD/VG

Staple tears

Abraded corner

Edge wear

Corner creases

Showcase #14, May-June 1958. © DC Comics.
Obvious defects: Numerous creases on spine and edges.
Hidden defects: Back cover poorly trimmed.
OWL: 9.

Abraded
corner

Numerous
stress lines

Corner
creases

Abraded
spine

Staple
tears

Numerous
spine
stress
lines

GD/VG

Corner
chip out

Significant wear on cover.
Very low reflectivity

Edge
creases

Corner
creases

Showcase #14
(Back cover)

Poorly trimmed
back cover

Amateur
repairs
evident

(2.0)   GOOD   (GD)

GRADE DESCRIPTION:
This grade shows substantial wear; often considered a "reading copy." Comics in this grade have all pages and covers, although there may be small pieces missing. Books in this grade are commonly creased, scuffed, abraded, soiled, but still completely readable.

COVER/EXTERIOR · Cover shows significant wear and may even be detached. Cover reflectivity is low and in some cases completely absent. Store stamp, name stamp, arrival date and initials are permitted. Book-length creases and dimples may be present. Rounded corners are more common. Moderate soiling, staining, discoloration and foxing may be present. The largest piece allowed missing from the front or back cover is usually a 1/2" triangle or a 1/4" square, although some Silver Age books such as 1960s Marvels have had the price corner box clipped from the top left front cover and may be considered Good if they would otherwise have graded higher. Tape and other forms of amateur repair are common in Silver Age and older books.

SPINE · Roll is likely. May have up to a 2" spine split.

STAPLES · Staples may be degraded, replaced or missing. Moderate staple tears and stress lines may be present, as well as rust migration.

PAPER/INTERIOR · Paper is brown but not brittle. A moderate acidic odor may be present. Centerfold may be loose or detached. Moderate interior tears may be present.

GD Some of the most collectable comic books are rarely found in better than GOOD condition. Most collectors consider this the lowest collectable grade because comic books in lesser condition are often incomplete and/or brittle. Traditionally, collectors have sometimes found it difficult to differentiate this grade from the next lower grade, FAIR. This task can be simplified if one remembers that a comic book in GOOD condition can have a moderate to large accumulation of defects but still preserves readability.

BINDERY/PRINTING
do not affect grade

COVER INKS/GLOSS
low, sometimes no reflectivity

COVER WEAR
significant wear,
may be detached

COVER CREASES
book-length creases or dimples

SOILING, STAINING
discoloration, fading, foxing,
or moderate soiling

DATES/STAMPS
do not affect grade

SPINE ROLL
roll likely

SPINE SPLIT
up to 2" split

STAPLES
degraded, replaced
or missing

STAPLE TEARS
moderate tears

RUST MIGRATION
may have migration

STRESS LINES
lines are common

CORNERS
rounded corners more common

CENTERFOLD
loose or detached

INTERIOR TEARS
moderate tears

PAPER QUALITY/COLOR
brown, not brittle

ACID ODOR
moderate odor

GD

MISSING PIECES
1/2" triangle, 1/4" square

AMATEUR REPAIRS
common in Silver Age and older

COUPON CUT
none allowed

READABILITY
preserved

Whiz Comics #9, October 1940. © Fawcett Publications.
Obvious defects: Cover corner piece missing.
Hidden defects: Blunted edges on some interior pages.
OWL: 5.

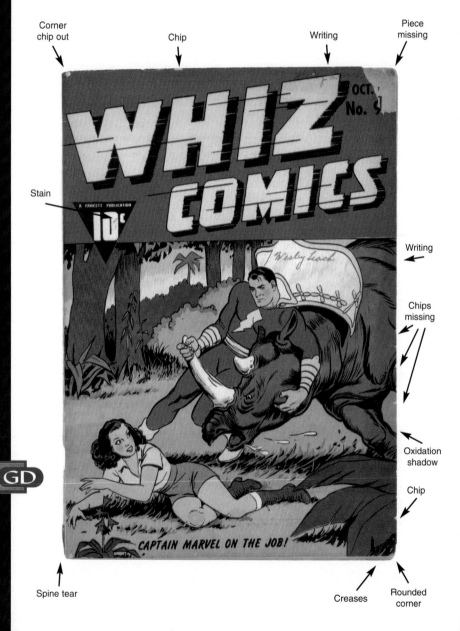

Corner chip out

Chip

Writing

Piece missing

Stain

Writing

Chips missing

Oxidation shadow

Chip

GD

Spine tear

Creases

Rounded corner

Looney Tunes and Merrie Melodies Comics #3, January 1942. © Warner Bros.
Obvious defects: Water stain with paper residue attached.
Hidden defects: None.
OWL: 7.

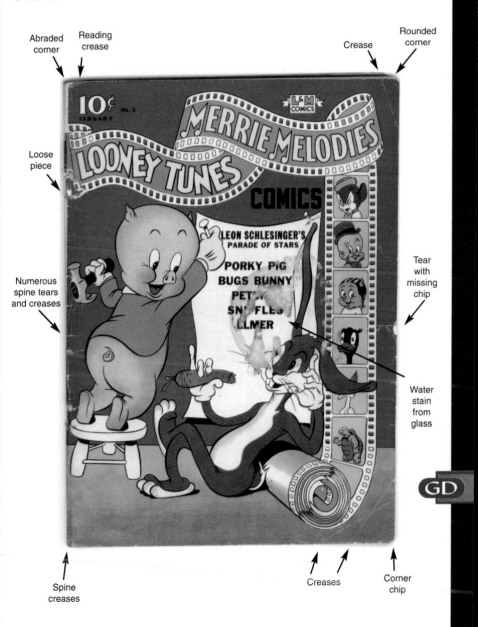

Abraded corner

Reading crease

Crease

Rounded corner

Loose piece

Numerous spine tears and creases

Tear with missing chip

Water stain from glass

GD

Spine creases

Creases

Corner chip

Air Ace Vol. 2 #1, January 1944. © Street and Smith Publications.
Obvious defects: Corner piece missing. Ink smudges and pencil marks.
Hidden defects: Some interior pages have brittle edges.
OWL: 5.

Edge tear   Edge tear   Ink smudges   Pencil mark   Corner chip

Ink smudges

Pencil marks

GD

Corner chip   Frayed edge   1/2" corner piece missing

The Flash #129, June 1962. © DC Comics.
Obvious defects: Large diagonal cover crease. Large piece missing from lower
left cover
Hidden defects: Spine roll.
OWL: 8.

Rounded corner

Long diagonal crease

Edge tear

Abraded spine

Tear

Chip

Split spine

GD

Missing corner piece

Loose piece

Wrinkled area

Corner creases

Superman #2, Fall 1939. © DC Comics.
Obvious defects: Tape on spine. Browning near edges.
Hidden defects: Brittle interior pages.
OWL: 5.

Amateur glue repair

Crease

Rounded corner

Tape on spine

Browning

Chip missing

Stains

Browning

GD

Low reflectivity

Spine split

Tear

Color flecks and chips

Rounded corner

No. 2

SUPERMAN

10¢

64 PAGES in COLOR!

Another complete book of the astounding adventures of the one and only
SUPERMAN!

Captain Marvel Adventures #5, December 1941. © Fawcett Publications.
Obvious defects: Two pieces missing from cover.
Hidden defects: None.
OWL: 6.

Corner
chip out

Piece missing

Color
scrape

Spine
loose at
staple

Animal
chew
extends
through
3/4 of all
pages

GD

Piece missing

Corner
crease

2.0 GOOD

Comics on Parade #35, January 1942. © United Features Syndicate.
Obvious defects: Out of register printing.
Hidden defects: Color flecking near spine. Rounded corners on interior pages.
OWL: 5.

Little Al of the F.B.I. #10, 1950. © Ziff-Davis.
Obvious defects: Rolled spine, worn edges and numerous creasings.
Hidden defects: Cover is wrinkled with brittle pages inside.
OWL: 6.

Abraded
corner

Dirt smudge and ink
on title letters

ink writing
on cover

Heavy edge
wear

Corner
chip

Edge
tear

Spine
tear

Long 4"
crease

Spine
tears

Color
flecks

Tears
around a
rusted
staple

Spine
roll

Long center
crease

GD

Walt Disney's Comics & Stories #146, November 1952. © Walt Disney Co.
Obvious defects: Numerous cover creases with color loss.
Hidden defects: Minor spine roll.
OWL: 9.

Cover creasing heaviest
along spine

Pen writing

Pencil
writing

Stress
marks

Blunted
edge

Pencil
writing
and ink
marks

GD

Rubbing
and
stress
marks

Significant
cover wear

Slightly
miswrapped
cover

Showcase #17, Nov.-Dec. 1958. © DC Comics.
Obvious defects: Spine is abraded and wrinkled. Numerous creases. Color loss in bottom left corner.
Hidden defects: Interior pages wrinkled.
OWL: **8.**

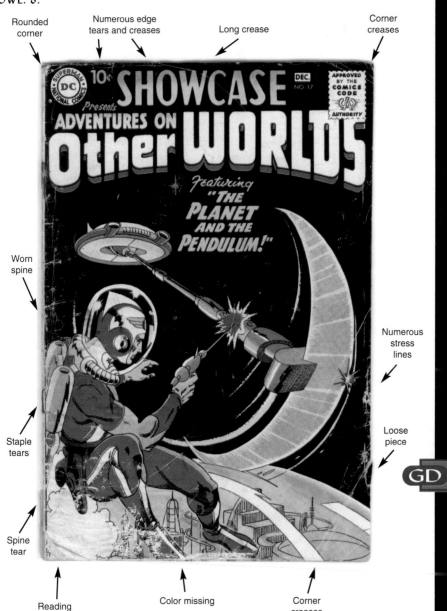

Rounded corner

Numerous edge tears and creases

Long crease

Corner creases

Worn spine

Numerous stress lines

Loose piece

Staple tears

Spine tear

GD

Reading creases

Color missing

Corner creases

Mystery in Space #71, November 1961. © DC Comics.
Obvious defects: Numerous creases and wrinkles.
Hidden defects: Light soiling. Pen indentations.
OWL: 9.

Abraded
corner

Wrinkled edge

Center crease

Crease

Abraded
spine

Spine
tear

Small
tears
along
edge

GD

Corner
crease

Corner chip with
color flecking

Crease

Color
flecking

Poorly trimmed
edge

Rounded
corner

Life With Archie #50, June 1966. © Archie Publications.
Obvious defects: Cover is detached. Cover has light soiling and stress lines.
Hidden defects: None.
OWL: 7.

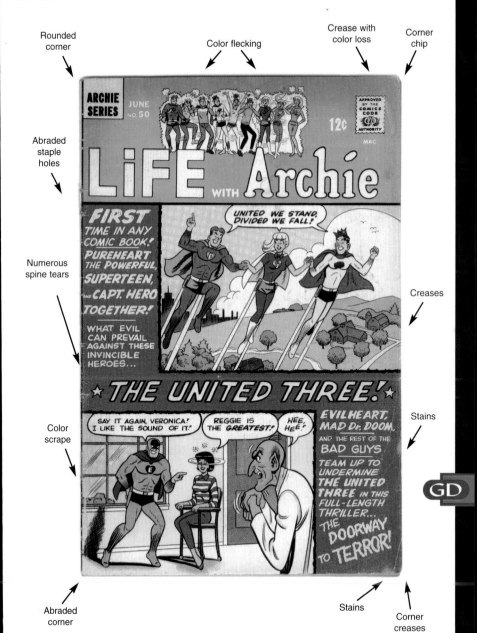

Rounded corner

Color flecking

Crease with color loss

Corner chip

Abraded staple holes

Numerous spine tears

Creases

Color scrape

Stains

GD

Abraded corner

Stains

Corner creases

Modern Love #2, Aug.-Sept. 1949. © William M. Gaines.
Obvious defects: Severely rusted staples. Water damage on spine. Abundant soiling.
Hidden defects: Loose centerfold and interior pages.
OWL: 5.

Abraded corner

Spine roll

Crease

Rounded corners

Rusted staple with rust migration

Chip

Foxing

Worn edge

Rusted staple

GD

Blunted corner

Modern Love #2
(Back cover)

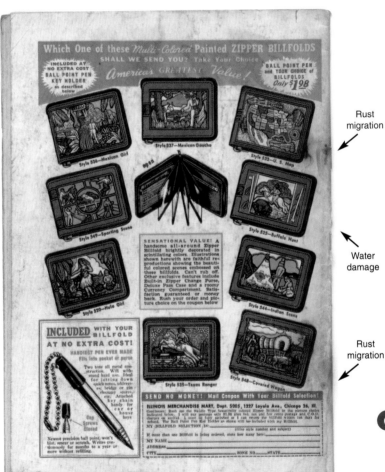

Rust migration

Water damage

Rust migration

Walt Disney's Comics and Stories #153, June 1953. © Walt Disney Company.
Obvious defects: Worn spine and abundant creases.
Hidden defects: Cover detached at upper staple.
Note: Subscription label does not affect grade.
OWL: 7.

Abraded
corner

Length-wide
crease

Small
pieces
missing

Worn
spine
with
moderate
tears

GD

Multiple
dimples
on cover

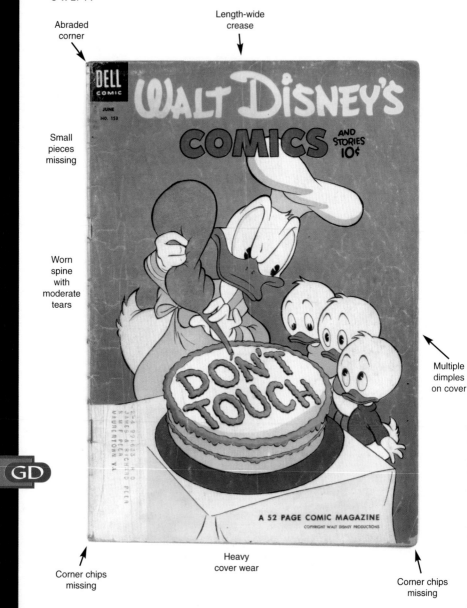

Corner chips
missing

Heavy
cover wear

Corner chips
missing

Peanuts #9, May-July 1961. © United Features Syndicate.
Obvious defects: Substantial writing on cover. Piece missing
Hidden defects: Slightly rusted staple.
OWL: 8.

Slightly
miswrapped
cover

Slightly
rusted
staple

Numerous
stress
lines

Rust
migration

Piece
missing

GD

Moderate
soiling

Light
crease

(1.5) FAIR/GOOD (FR/GD)

GRADE DESCRIPTION:
A comic showing substantial to heavy wear. A copy in this grade still has all pages and covers, although there may be pieces missing. Books in this grade are commonly creased, scuffed, abraded, soiled, and possibly unattractive, but still generally readable.

COVER/EXTERIOR · Cover shows considerable wear and may be detached. Almost no cover reflectivity remaining. Store stamp, name stamp, arrival date and initials are permitted. Book-length creases, tears and folds may be present. Rounded corners are increasingly common. Soiling, staining, discoloration and foxing is generally present. Up to 1/10 of the back cover may be missing. Tape and other forms of amateur repair are increasingly common in Silver Age and older books.

SPINE · Roll is common. May have a spine split between 2" and 2/3 the length of the book.

STAPLES · Staples may be degraded, replaced or missing. Staple tears and stress lines are common, as well as rust migration.

PAPER/INTERIOR · Paper is brown and may show brittleness around the edges. Acidic odor may be present. Centerfold may be loose or detached. Interior tears are common.

BINDERY/PRINTING
do not affect grade

COVER INKS/GLOSS
almost no reflectivity

COVER WEAR
considerable wear,
may be detached

COVER CREASES
creases, tears, and folds

SOILING, STAINING
generally present

DATES/STAMPS
do not affect grade

SPINE ROLL
roll common

SPINE SPLIT
between 2" and 2/3 length

STAPLES
degraded, replaced,
one missing

STAPLE TEARS
tears are common

RUST MIGRATION
may have migration

STRESS LINES
lines are common

CORNERS
rounded corners
increasingly common

CENTERFOLD
loose or detached

INTERIOR TEARS
tears are common

PAPER QUALITY/COLOR
brown, edges show brittleness

ACID ODOR
odor present

MISSING PIECES
up to 1/10 of the
back cover missing

AMATEUR REPAIRS
increasingly common in
Silver Age and older

FR/GD

COUPON CUT
none allowed

READABILITY
generally preserved

Action Comics #17, October 1939. © DC Comics.
Obvious defects: 3 inch tear out from spine. Browning on cover edges.
Hidden defects: Spine split from bottom to lower staple.
OWL: 4.

Corner chip out

Corner creases

Rounded corner

Browning

Corner crease

Browning

Writing

Frayed spine

Frayed edge

Color chip out

3 inch tear

Edge wear

FR/GD

2" spine split

Rounded corner

Special Edition Comics #1, August 1940. © Fawcett Publications.
Obvious defects: Cover pieces missing and cover soiling.
Hidden defects: Mold spots and staining.
OWL: 6.

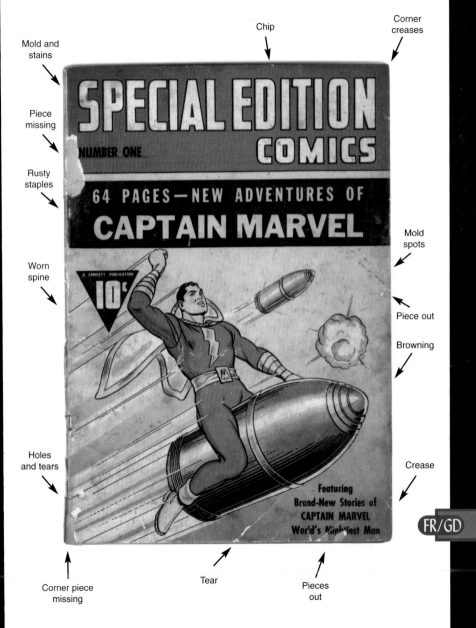

Chip

Corner
creases

Mold and
stains

Piece
missing

Rusty
staples

Worn
spine

Mold
spots

Piece out

Browning

Holes
and tears

Crease

FR/GD

Corner piece
missing

Tear

Pieces
out

New York World's Fair Comics, 1940. © DC Comics.
Obvious defects: Squarebound spine is heavily worn.
Hidden defects: Brittle pages.
OWL: 4.

Chip missing

Numerous creases

Chip missing

Abraded corner

Tape residue

Pencil marks

Cover soiling

Pencil marks

Color flecks

FR/GD

Abraded corner

Missing pieces

Numerous tears

Corner creases and abrasion

New York World's Fair Comics 1940
(Back cover)

Abraded
corner

Numerous
creases

Tape
residue

Numerous
chips
missing

Tear

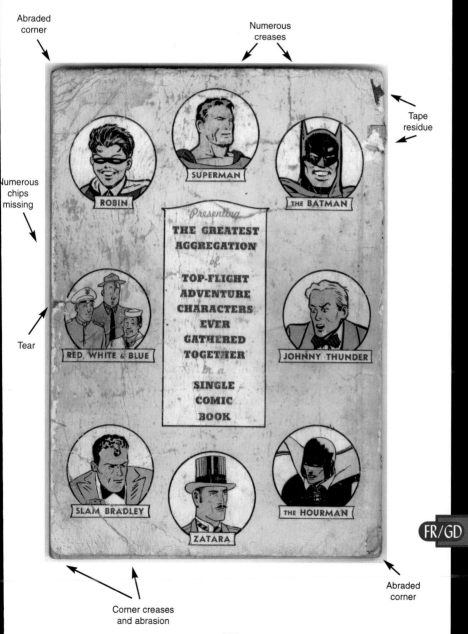

FR/GD

Abraded
corner

Corner creases
and abrasion

Air Fighters Comics Volume 2 #10, Fall 1945. © Hillman Periodicals.
Obvious defects: Worn spine and corners. Water stains on cover.
Hidden defects: Loose centerfold.
OWL: 7.

Abraded corner

Frayed edge

Rounded corner

Pencil marks

Water stains

Worn spine

Tape on spine

FR/GD

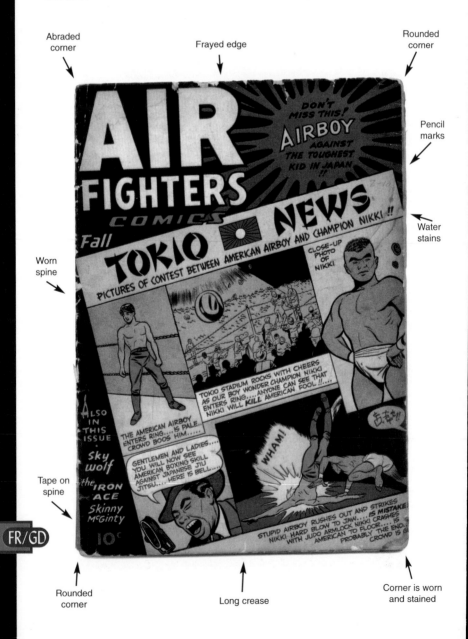

Rounded corner

Long crease

Corner is worn and stained

Shock SuspenStories #17, Oct.-Nov. 1954. © William M. Gaines.
Obvious defects: Excessive cover creases and spine wear. Writing on cover.
Hidden defects: Loose interior pages.
OWL: 4.

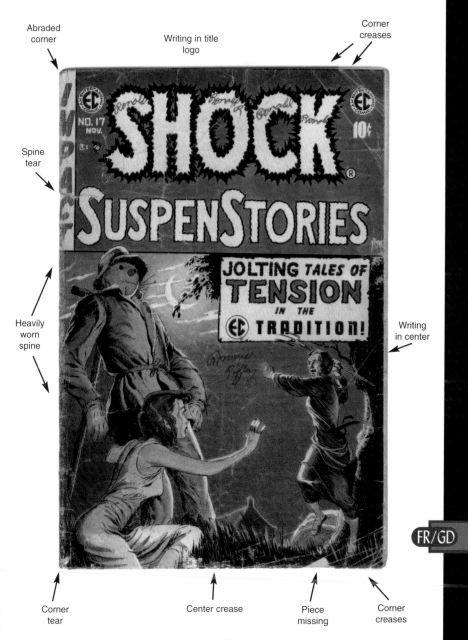

Abraded
corner

Writing in title
logo

Corner
creases

Spine
tear

Heavily
worn
spine

Writing
in center

Corner
tear

Center crease

Piece
missing

Corner
creases

FR/GD

Poppo of the Popcorn Theatre #1, 1955. © George Gale.
Obvious defects: Large piece missing from cover.
Hidden defects: None.
OWL: 8.

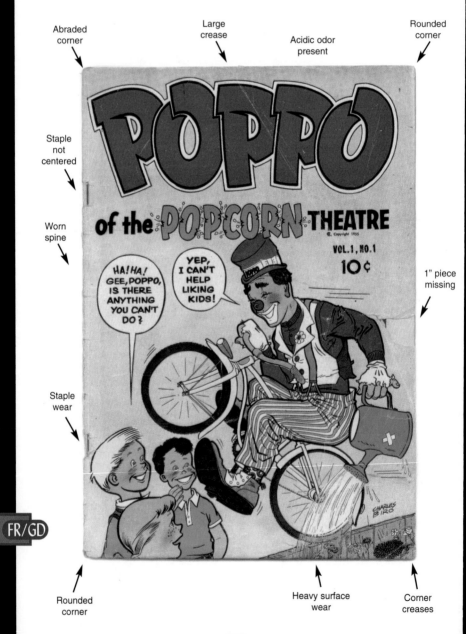

Abraded corner

Large crease

Acidic odor present

Rounded corner

Staple not centered

Worn spine

1" piece missing

Staple wear

FR/GD

Rounded corner

Heavy surface wear

Corner creases

Showcase #3, July-August 1956. © DC Comics.
Obvious defects: Heavy color loss and spine damage.
Hidden defects: Wrinkled interior pages.
OWL: 7.
Note: Mildew smell is obvious.

Abraded
corner

Heavy color loss

Numerous
stress lines

Corner
creases

Staple
tears

Color
loss

Abraded
spine

Large
crease

Staple
tears

FR/GD

Rounded corner

Corner
creases

Super Duck #21, August 1958. © Archie Publications.
Obvious defects: Excessive staining and bundling creases
Hidden defects: Loose inner pages.
OWL: 5.

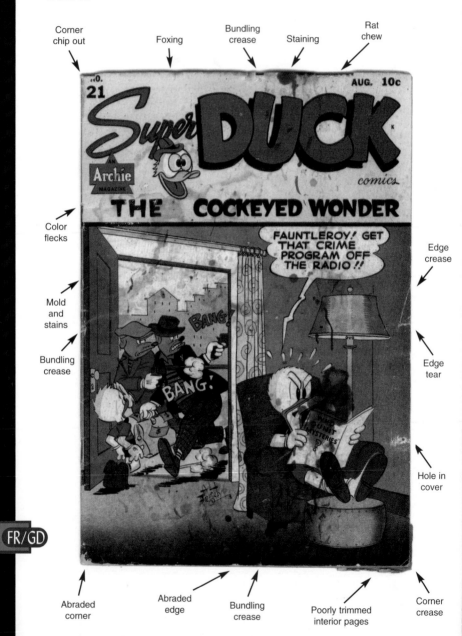

Corner chip out · Foxing · Bundling crease · Staining · Rat chew

Color flecks · Mold and stains · Bundling crease

Edge crease · Edge tear · Hole in cover

Abraded corner · Abraded edge · Bundling crease · Poorly trimmed interior pages · Corner crease

FR/GD

The Avengers #9, October 1964. © Marvel Characters, Inc.
Obvious defects: Stress lines at top of cover. Abraded corners. Spine split.
1/10th of the back cover missing.
Hidden defects: Brittle pages.
OWL: 4.

Abraded
corner

Numerous
stress lines

Corner
creases

1 1/2"
spine split

Spine
creases

Foxing

Rusty
staple

Abraded
corner

Edge
tears

Multiple dimples
and stress lines
on cover

Corner
creases

FR/GD

The Incredible Hulk #103, May, 1968. © Marvel Characters, Inc.
Obvious defects: Worn spine and ragged edges.
Hidden defects: Loose interior pages.
OWL: 7.

Abraded corner

Reading creases

Numerous stress lines

Soiling on white title letters

Loose interior pages

Foxing

Issue no. digit cut

Numerous stress lines

Large dimple at center of cover

Numerous stress lines

Tears around staple

2 1/2" long crease

FR/GD

Abraded corner

Chipping

Abraded corner

Issue no.
digit cut

The Incredible Hulk #103
(Back cover)

2" tear

Abraded
corner

Abraded
corner

(1.0)   FAIR   (FR)

GRADE DESCRIPTION:
A copy in this grade shows heavy wear. Some collectors consider this the lowest collectible grade because comic books in lesser condition are usually incomplete and/or brittle. Comics in this grade are usually soiled, faded, ragged and possibly unattractive. This is the last grade in which a comic remains generally readable.

COVER/EXTERIOR - Cover may be detached, and inks have lost all reflectivity. Creases, tears and/or folds are prevalent. Corners are commonly rounded or absent. Soiling and staining is present. Books in this condition generally have all pages and most of the covers, although there may be up to 1/4 of the front cover missing or no back cover, but not both. Tape and other forms of amateur repair are more common.

SPINE - Spine roll is more common; spine split can extend up to 2/3 the length of the book.

STAPLES - Staples may be missing or show rust and discoloration. An accumulation of staple tears and stress lines may be present, as well as rust migration.

PAPER/INTERIOR - Paper is brown and may show brittleness around the edges but not in the central portion of the pages. Acidic odor may be present. Accumulation of interior tears. Chunks may be missing. The centerfold may be missing if readability is generally preserved (although there may be difficulty). Coupons may be cut.

Demand for comics in this grade from the 1930s through the 1960s is high, but FR books should be examined for brittleness. Some POOR condition books have missing pages replaced with pages from a different issue or title to give the appearance of a FAIR book.

BINDERY/PRINTING	COVER INKS/GLOSS
do not affect grade	no reflectivity

COVER WEAR	COVER CREASES
may be detached	creases, tears and folds

SOILING, STAINING	DATES/STAMPS
present	do not affect grade

SPINE ROLL	SPINE SPLIT
roll more common	up to 2/3 length

STAPLES	STAPLE TEARS	RUST MIGRATION
may be missing	accumulation of tears	may have migration

STRESS LINES	CORNERS
accumulation of lines	rounded or absent

CENTERFOLD	INTERIOR TEARS
may be missing	accumulation of tears

PAPER QUALITY/COLOR	ACID ODOR
brown, edges show brittleness	odor present

MISSING PIECES	AMATEUR REPAIRS
up to 1/4 front cover or entire back cover, and/or chunks	more common

COUPON CUT	READABILITY
coupon may be cut	generally preserved to difficulty

More Fun Comics #15, November 1936. © DC Comics.
Obvious defects: Poorly trimmed right edge. Staples replaced, centerfold detached. Coupon cut inside. No reflectivity on cover.
Hidden defects: Color touch.
OWL: 5.

Frayed edge

Poorly retrimmed edge

3" spine split

Untrimmed interior page

Soiling

Ink stains

Soiling

Staples replaced

Frayed edge

Crease

Corner creases

Abraded corner

Color touch

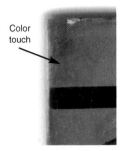

More Fun Comics #15
(Back cover)

Color touch

Walt Disney's Comics and Stories #1, October 1940. © Walt Disney Company.
Obvious defects: Cover chunk missing. Rusted staples. Coupon cut on back cover.
Hidden defects: Torn interior pages. Water damage on back cover.
OWL: 5.

Chunk
missing

Back
cover
spine

Multiple
spine
stress
lines

Rusted
staple

Spine
chips

Rusted
staple

Large
stain

True Comics #2, June 1941. © The Parents' Institute.
Obvious defects: Taped spine. Edge chips and tears. Center crease.
Hidden defects: None.
OWL: 4.

Tape along spine

Chips

Worn spine

Tears

Chips

Tape along spine

Some brittleness along edge

6" crease

Rounded corner

FR

Tom & Jerry Comics #76, November 1940. © Loew's Inc.
Obvious defects: Heavy creasing.
Hidden defects: Vertical tears on top of interior pages
OWL: 7.

Abraded
corner

Worn
spine

Staple is
rusty
and not
centered

Heavy
creases
and
crumpling

Heavy
creases
and
crumpling

FR

Heavy
creases

Heavily
blunted
edge

Heavy
creases

Wedding Bells #1. February 1954. © Comic Magazines.
Obvious defects: 7" spine split. Water stains on outer and inner covers.
Hidden defects: Small tears on some interior pages.
OWL: 8.

The Flash #232, March-April 1975. © DC Comics.
Obvious defects: Well worn cover attached by tape. Back cover missing.
Hidden defects: Coupon cut and crossword puzzle filled in with pencil.
OWL: 8.

Corner creases

Frayed edge

Tear

Tape

Edge tears

Tape

Frayed edge

Spine tears

FR

Abraded corner

Frayed edge with heavy surface wear

Rounded corner

The Flash #232
(Back of book
showing
last page -
back cover
missing)

Stalker #1, June-July 1975. © DC Comics.
Obvious defects: Substantial cat chew damage on front and back covers.
Hidden defects: Small tears and holes on interior pages.
OWL: 8.

Crease

Corner
creases

Staple
tear

Numerous
creases
and stress
lines

Cat chew

Crease

Crease

Cat chew

Buffy the Vampire Slayer #9, May 1999. © 20th Century Fox.
Obvious defects: Massive cover abrasion/tear with underlying damage extending through 10 interior pages. Spine creases
Hidden defects: None.
OWL: Not applicable.

Massive
cover trauma

Close-up on
first interior
page

Spine
creases

Spine
creases

Numerous
diagonal folds

(0.5) POOR (PR)

GRADE DESCRIPTION:
Most comic books in this grade have been sufficiently degraded to the point where there is little or no collector value; they are easily identified by a complete absence of eye appeal. Comics in this grade are brittle almost to the point of turning to dust with a touch, and are usually incomplete.

COVER/EXTERIOR - Extreme fading may render the cover almost indiscernible. May have extremely severe stains, mildew or heavy cover abrasion to the point that some cover inks are indistinct/absent. Covers may be detached with large chunks missing. Can have extremely ragged edges and extensive creasing. Corners are rounded or virtually absent. Covers may have been defaced with paints, varnishes, glues, oil, indelible markers or dyes, and may have suffered heavy water damage. Can also have extensive amateur repairs such as laminated covers.

SPINE - Extreme roll present; can have extremely ragged spines or a complete, book-length split.

STAPLES - Staples can be missing or show extreme rust and discoloration. Extensive staple tears and stress lines may be present, as well as extreme rust migration.

PAPER/INTERIOR - Paper exhibits moderate to severe brittleness (where the comic book literally falls apart when examined). Extreme acidic odor may be present. Extensive interior tears. Multiple pages, including the centerfold, may be missing that affect readability. Coupons may be cut.

COVERLESS COMICS - The exception to the "not collectible in POOR" rule. Many collectors want clean, readable, coverless comics that are priced fairly. Coverless copies of key and/or rare comics are often in demand by collectors. These enthusiasts also seek coverless comics to retrieve centerfolds, first wraparounds, coupons and even staples in order to restore other copies of the same or a similar incomplete comic.

INCOMPLETE/UNCOLLECTABLE - At the very bottom of the range, comics with the absolute maximum number of defects, heavy degradation, and significant portions of the book missing might not even be considered Poor any longer, but may be termed "incomplete." These books are so ruined as to be rendered unreadable and virtually uncollectable.

BINDERY/PRINTING	COVER INKS/GLOSS
do not affect grade	extreme fading

COVER WEAR	COVER CREASES
detached with chunks missing	extreme creases, ragged edges

SOILING, STAINING	DATES/STAMPS
extreme soiling, staining and discoloration	do not affect grade

SPINE ROLL	SPINE SPLIT
extreme roll	extremely ragged or completely split

STAPLES	STAPLE TEARS	RUST MIGRATION
missing or extremely rusted, discolored	extensive tears	extreme migration

STRESS LINES	CORNERS
many lines	rounded or absent

CENTERFOLD	INTERIOR TEARS
may be missing	extensive tears

PAPER QUALITY/COLOR	ACID ODOR
moderate to severe brittleness	extreme odor

MISSING PIECES	AMATEUR REPAIRS
large chunks of front cover and back cover, and/or interior	extensive repairs

COUPON CUT	READABILITY
coupon(s) may be cut	multiple pages missing

PR

Wonder Comics Vol. 2 #2, July 1945. © Great Publications.
Obvious defects: Substantial water damage and discoloration. Text from other publication transfered onto cover. Cover surface is wrinkled.
Hidden defects: Water damage and discoloration on inside pages.
OWL: 4.

Paper remnant
glued to cover

Foxing

Numerous stains
on title logo

Corner
chip

Color
flecks

Torn
spine

Rusted
spine

Color
loss

Extensive
color loss

Corner
chip

Wonder Comics Vol. 2 #2
(Back cover)

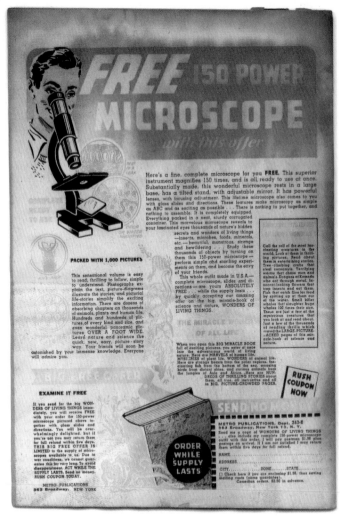

Pogo Possum #8, January-March 1952. © Walt Kelly.
Obvious defects: Substantial water damage and discoloration. Staples are rusted
and rust migration is evident. Paper is wrinkled.
Hidden defects: Water damage and discoloration on inside pages.
OWL: 8.

Severely
rusted
staple

Severely
rusted
staple

Incomplete cover
from water damage

Discoloration

Pogo Possum #8
(Back cover)

Discoloration

Discoloration

Incomplete cover
from water damage

Walt Disney's Comics and Stories #158, November 1953. © Walt Disney Co.
Obvious defects: Water damage. White mold along edges.
Hidden defects: Wrinkled interior pages.
OWL: 9.

Discoloration

White mold from
water damage

Folded corner
creases

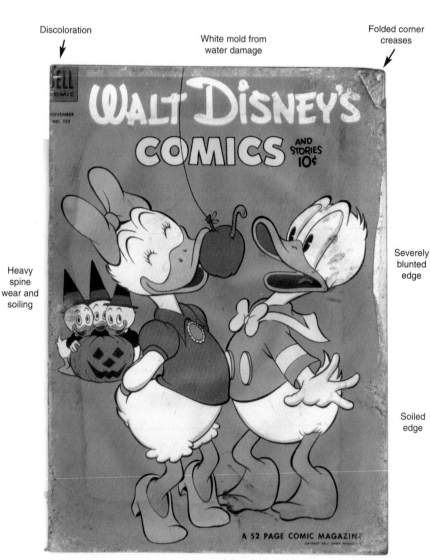

Heavy
spine
wear and
soiling

Severely
blunted
edge

Soiled
edge

Heavy edge wear
and soiling

Marvel Two-In-One #4, July 1974. © Marvel Characters, Inc.
Obvious defects: Coverless.
Hidden defects: Coupon cut affecting readability.
OWL: 7.

Although this book contains a plethora of examples of most grades in the 10 Point Scale, it's difficult to visualize the degradation that takes place as you move from the best example of a given comic to the worst copy. To demonstrate this progression, we've taken one specific comic

book - DC Comics' **The Atom #25** - and presented it here in conditions ranging from 9.0 to 1.0, to further illustrate how a comic might degrade as it moves down the major steps of the 10 Point Scale. Who better than the Atom to aid us with this quick visual guide to the amazing shrinking scale?

9.0 Very Fine/Near Mint VF/NM

Slight
staple
stress
lines

Slight
staple
stress
lines

High cover reflectivity

Slight edge
wear

© DC Comics

Minor
spine
wear

Slight
staple
stress
lines

Slight
staple
stress
lines

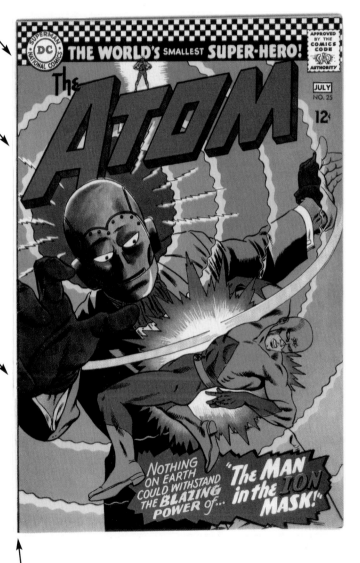

Minor
spine
wear

335

Corner
wear

1/8" light
crease

Light
spine
wear

Staple
stress
lines

Light spine
wear along
spine

1/8" light
crease

Cover travelled

Corner wear

Staples not centered

Stress lines

Cover indentations

Minor corner tear

Blunted corner

337

1/8" minor corner crease

Minor edge wear

Cover indentations

Staple stress lines

Spine stress

Staple stress

Spine stress

Moderate wear

Cover indentations

4.0 Very Good VG

Cover travelled

Cover inks have low reflectivity

Rounded corner

Staples not centered

Edge wear

Numerous spine stress lines

Rounded corner

Surface has multiple dimples and general wear

1/4" moderate crease

Rounded corner

© DC Comics

Cover shows
substantial wear

Rusted
staple

Edge
wear

Spine
stress
and
tears

Browning

Corner
wear

Edge wear

Corner
creases

Cover has low reflectivity and
numerous dimples and overall
cover wear

© DC Comics

Corner wear

Significant wear on cover

Rounded corner

Color fleck

Edge wear

Moderate spine wear

Pencil marks

Staple tears

Creases

1/8" color scrape

Corner wear

Cover has low reflectivity and numerous dimples

Spine roll

Center crease

Cover shows heavy wear

Color fleck

Corner wear

Heavy spine wear

2" spine split

Staple tears

Edge wear

Long crease

Corner crease

1 1/2" piece missing

Color scraped

Corner crease

THE WORLD'S SMALLEST SUPER-HERO!

The ATOM

JULY NO. 25

12¢

NOTHING ON EARTH COULD WITHSTAND THE BLAZING POWER OF... "The MAN in the ION MASK!"

Comic Book Cover Index

Glossary

ABRADED CORNER - Grinding of corner area caused by improper handling or storage.

ABRADED STAPLE HOLE - See **Staple Hole**.

AD - Abbreviation for **Arrival Date**.

ADZINE - A magazine primarily devoted to the advertising of comic books and collectibles as its first publishing priority as opposed to written articles.

ALLENTOWN COLLECTION - A collection discovered in 1987-88 just outside Allentown, Pennsylvania. The Allentown collection consisted of 135 Golden Age comics, characterized by high grade and superior paper quality.

ANILINE - A poisonous oily liquid, colorless when pure, obtained from coal tar and especially from nitro benzene, used in making inks, dyes and perfumes; also found in certain medicines, plastics, resins, etc. The oxidation of aniline produces quinone, which can cause transfer stains and paper discoloration. See **Quinone**.

ANNUAL - (1) A book that is published yearly; (2) Can also refer to some square bound comics.

APO - Abbreviation for Ad Page Out.

ARRIVAL DATE - The date written (often in pencil) or stamped on the cover of comics by either the local wholesaler, newsstand owner, or distributor. The date precedes the cover date by approximately 15 to 75 days, and may vary considerably from one locale to another or from one year to another.

ASHCAN - A publisher's in-house facsimile of a proposed new title. Most ashcans have black and white covers stapled to an existing coverless comic on the inside; other ashcans are totally black and white. In modern parlance, it can also refer to promotional or sold comics, often smaller than standard comic size and usually in black and white, released by publishers to advertise the forthcoming arrival of a new title or story.

AT - Abbreviation for Archival safe Tape.

ATOM AGE - Comics published from approximately 1946-1956.

BACK-UP FEATURE - A story or character that usually appears after the main feature in a comic book; often not featured on the cover.

BAD GIRL ART - A term popularized in the early '90s to describe an attitude as well as a style of art that portrays women in a sexual and often action-oriented way.

BAXTER PAPER - A high quality, heavy, white paper used in the printing of some comics.

BBC - Abbreviation for Bottom of Back Cover.

BC - Abbreviation for Back Cover.

BI-MONTHLY - Published every two months.

BI-WEEKLY - Published every two weeks.

BINDER - The person that oversees the bindery process.

BINDER HOLES - Either two or three holes punched into the spine of comics in order to fit them into a two or three ring binder.

BINDER PERFS - See **Perforations**.

BINDERY - The location where comic books are assembled, trimmed, and stapled and/or glued.

BINDERY CORNER - Small, triangular spine corner tears that occur during binding.

BINDERY DEFECT - Defects associated with the binding process, including mistrimming, miswrapping, inaccurate stapling, etc.

BINDERY TRIMMING DEFECT TAXONOMY - Comic is not cut/trimmed correctly at the bindery.

Type I - Cover cut squarely:

I a - Cover square; rectangular part of back cover shows along spine or right edge of front or back cover.

I b - Cover square; triangular part of back cover shows along spine or right edge of front or back cover.

I c - Cover square; white unprinted rectangular strip shows along top or bottom of front or back cover, indicating that cover travelled before trimming.

I d - Cover square; white unprinted triangular strip shows along top or bottom of front or back cover, indicating that cover travelled before trimming.

Type 2 - Cover not cut squarely:

2a, 2b, 2c, 2d - Cover not square; otherwise same as above.

2e - Cover not square; no other defects.

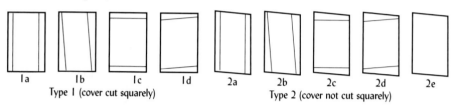

Type I (cover cut squarely)   Type 2 (cover not cut squarely)

BLACK COVER - A comic cover where black is the predominant color. These covers more readily show wear. Because they rarely occur in high grade, black covers are in great demand by collectors.

BLUNTED CORNER - See **Corner Blunting.**

BONDAGE COVER - Usually denotes a female in bondage.

BOUND COPY - A comic that has been bound into a book. The process requires that the spine be trimmed and sometimes sewn into a book-like binding.

BOUND SHORT - See **Siamese Pages.**

BRITISH ISSUE - A comic printed for distribution in Great Britain; these copies sometimes have the price listed in pence or pounds instead of cents or dollars.

BRITTLENESS - A severe condition of paper deterioration where paper loses its flexibility and thus chips and/or flakes easily.

BRN - Abbreviation for Brown.

BRONZE AGE - Comics published from approximately 1970 through 1985.

BROWNING - (1) The aging of paper characterized by the ever-increasing level of oxidation characterized by darkening; (2) The level of paper deterioration one step more severe than tanning and one step before brittleness.

BRT - Abbreviation for Brittle.

BUG - Abbreviation for Bug Chew.

CAMEO - The brief appearance of one character in the strip of another.

CANADIAN ISSUE - A comic printed for distribution in Canada; these copies sometimes have no advertising.

CC - Abbreviation for **Coupon Cut.**

CCA - Abbreviation for **Comics Code Authority.**

CE - Abbreviation for Canadian Edition.

CENTER CREASE - See **Subscription Copy.**

CENTERFOLD or CENTER SPREAD - The two folded pages in the center of a comic book at the terminal end of the staples.

CERTIFIED GRADING - A process provided by a professional grading service that certifies a given grade for a comic and seals the book in a protective Slab.

CF - Abbreviation for Centerfold.

CFL - Abbreviation for Centerfold Loose.

CFO - Abbreviation for Centerfold Out.

CGC - Abbreviation for the certified comic book grading company, Comics Guaranty, LLC.

CHIP CUT - Missing piece smaller than 1 square millimeter.

CHP - Abbreviation for edge Chipping.

CIRCULATION COPY - See Subscription Copy.

CIRCULATION FOLD - See Subscription Fold.

CL - Abbreviation for Cover Loose.

CLASSIC COVER - A cover considered by collectors to be highly desirable because of its subject matter, artwork, historical importance, etc.

CLEANING - A process in which dirt and dust is removed.

CO - Abbreviation for Cut Out.

COCKLING - Bubbling on the surface of the comic book cover.

COLOR FLAKE - The color layer has been lost, making the white paper substrata visible. Color flakes are larger than 1 square millimeter and smaller than 2 square millimeters.

COLOR FLECK - The color layer has been lost, making the white paper substrata visible. Color flecks are no larger than 1 square millimeter.

COLOR TOUCH - A restoration process by which colored ink is used to hide color flecks, color flakes, and larger areas of missing color. Short for Color Touch-Up.

COMIC BOOK DEALER - (1) A seller of comic books; (2) One who makes a living buying and selling comic books.

COMIC BOOK REPAIR - When a tear, loose staple or centerfold has been mended without changing or adding to the original finish of the book. Repair may involve tape, glue or nylon gossamer, and is easily detected; it is considered a defect.

COMICS CODE AUTHORITY - A voluntary organization comprised of comic book publishers formed in 1954 to review (and possibly censor) comic books before they were printed and distributed. The emblem of the CCA is a white stamp in the upper right hand corner of comics dated after February 1955. The term "post-Code" refers to the time after this practice started, or approximately 1955 to the present.

COMPLETE RUN - All issues of a given title.

CON - A convention or public gathering of fans.

CONDITION - The state of preservation of a comic book, often inaccurately used interchangeably with Grade.

CORNER BLUNTING - Compression folds at approximately 45 degrees to the ends and sides of the comic, as if the corner of the comic were dropped against a hard surface.

CORNER CREASE - Permanent crease located within 1" of a corner, usually the upper right hand or lower right hand corner.

CORNER FOLD - A linear dent indicating folding within 1" of the corner, usually the upper right hand or lower right hand corner.

COSMIC AEROPLANE COLLECTION - A collection from Salt Lake City, Utah discovered by Cosmic Aeroplane Books, characterized by the moderate to high grade copies of 1930s-40s comics with pencil check marks in the margins of inside pages. It is thought that these comics were kept by a commercial illustration school and the check marks were placed beside panels that instructors wanted students to draw.

COSTUMED HERO - A costumed crime fighter with "developed" human powers instead of super powers.

COUPON CUT or COUPON MISSING - A coupon has been neatly removed with scissors or razor blade from the interior or exterior of the comic as opposed to having been ripped out.

COVER GLOSS - The reflective quality of the cover inks.

COVER LOOSE - (1) Cover has become completely detached from the staples; (2) Cover moves around on the staples but is not completely detached.

COVER MISSING - See Coverless.

COVER OFF - Cover is completely detached from the staples.

COVER REATTACHED - Cover has been repaired/restored to hold staples and reattached to comic interior.

COVER TRIMMED - Cover has been reduced in size by neatly cutting away rough or damaged edges.

COVERLESS - A comic with no cover attached. There is a niche demand for coverless comics, particularly in the case of hard-to-find key books otherwise impossible to locate intact. See Remainders.

C/P - Abbreviation for Cleaned and Pressed.

CREASE - A fold which causes ink removal, usually resulting in a white line. See Corner Crease and Reading Crease.

CRN - Abbreviation for Corner.

CROSSOVER - A story where one character appears prominently in the story of another character. See X-Over.

CRS - Abbreviation for Crease.

CT - Abbreviation for Color Touch.

CVLS - Abbreviation for Coverless.

CVR - Abbreviation for Cover.

DATE STAMP - Arrival or other date printed in ink somewhere in or on the comic by use of a stamp and stamp pad.

DBL - Abbreviation for Double.

DEALER - See Comic Book Dealer.

DEACIDIFICATION - Several different processes that reduce acidity in paper.

DEBUT - The first time that a character appears anywhere.

DEFECT - Any fault or flaw that detracts from perfection.

DEFECTIVES - Comics which, through flaws, are imperfect.

DEFORMED STAPLE - A staple that has not penetrated all the pages properly or is bent and/or misshapen. See Shallow Staple.

DENT - An indentation, usually on the cover, that does not penetrate the paper nor remove any material or gloss.

DENVER COLLECTION - A collection consisting primarily of early 1940s high grade number one issues bought at auction in Pennsylvania by a Denver, Colorado dealer.

DIE-CUT COVER - A comic book cover with areas or edges precut by a printer to a special shape or to create a desired effect.

DIMPLE - A surface indentation on the cover, usually caused by excessive thumb/finger pressure at the edge of the cover.

DIRT - Inorganic and organic substances that can be removed from paper by cleaning.

DISTRIBUTOR STRIPES - Color brushed or sprayed on the edges of comic book stacks by the distributor/wholesaler to code them for expedient exchange at the sales racks. Typical colors are red, orange, yellow, green, blue, and purple. Distributor stripes are not a defect.

DMP - Abbreviation for **Dimple**.

DOG - Abbreviation for Dog-eared.

DOUBLE - A duplicate copy of the same comic book.

DOUBLE COVER - When two covers are stapled to the comic interior instead of the usual one; the exterior cover often protects the interior cover from wear and damage. This is considered a desirable situation by some collectors and may increase collector value; this is not considered a defect.

DRUG PROPAGANDA STORY - A comic that makes an editorial stand about drug use.

DRUG USE STORY - A comic that shows the actual use of drugs: needle use, tripping, harmful effects, etc.

DRY PRESS - Machine used to flatten comics with rolled spines and/or folds.

DS - Abbreviation for **Dust Shadow**.

DUOTONE - Printed with black and one other color of ink. This process was common in comics printed in the 1930s.

DUST SHADOW - Darker, usually linear area at the edge of some comics stored in stacks. Some portion of the cover was not covered by the comic immediately above it and it was exposed to settling dust particles. Also see **Oxidation Shadow** and **Sun Shadow**.

EDGAR CHURCH COLLECTION - See **Mile High Collection**.

EMBOSSED COVER - A comic book cover with a pattern, shape or image pressed into the cover from the inside, creating a raised area.

ENCAPSULATION - Refers to the process of sealing certified comics in a protective plastic enclosure. Also see "slabbing."

ENTROPY - An inescapable fact of the physical universe, and the primary enemy of comic book collectors; basically, all ordered systems, including living things, have a tendency to break down and deteriorate over time. Fight it all you like with Mylar and backing boards, but entropy claims all things in the end.

ERASER MARK - Damage left when pencil marks are removed from the cover or inside of a comic; most identifiable when cover gloss is dulled.

EXT - Abbreviation for Extensive.

EXTENDERS - See **Staple Extenders**.

EYE APPEAL - A term which refers to the overall look of a comic book when held at approximately arm's length. A comic may have nice eye appeal yet still possess defects which reduce grade.

FADING - Loss of color due to exposure to sunlight or certain fluorescent lights which give off a moderate to high percentage of ultraviolet light.

FANNED PAGES - A condition caused by a rolled spine which progressively pulls interior pages away from the edge, creating a fanned appearance.

FANZINE - An amateur fan publication.

FC - Abbreviation for Front Cover.

FIBER FURNISH - The fibrous composition of the paper pulp.

FILE COPY - A high grade comic originating from the publisher's file; contrary to what some might believe, not all file copies are in Gem Mint condition. An arrival date on the cover of a comic does not indicate that it is a file copy, though a copyright date may.

FINGER OILS - Natural oils from the skin left when handling comics with bare hands; oil accelerates the collection of dust and dirt.

FIRST APPEARANCE - See **Debut**.

FLASHBACK - When a previous story is recalled.

FLE - Abbreviation for color Flecking.

FLECK - See **Color Fleck**.

FOIL COVER - A comic book cover that has had a thin metallic foil hot stamped on it. Many of these "gimmick" covers date from the early '90s, and might include chromium, prism and hologram covers as well.

FOLDING ERROR - A bindery defect in which the comic is folded off-center, resulting in part of the front cover appearing on the back cover, or more seriously, part of the back cover appearing on the front cover.

FOLDED OFF-CENTER - See **Folding Error**.

FOLDS - Linear dents in paper that do not result in the loss of ink; not a crease.

FOLIO - A sheet of paper, folded once in the middle, making 2 leaves or 4 pages; 32 interior pages are made up of 8 folios. The centerfold, cover, and first wraparound are examples of folios.

FOUR COLOR - Series of comics produced by Dell, characterized by hundreds of different features; named after the four color process of printing. See **One Shot**.

FOUR COLOR PROCESS - The process of printing with the three primary colors (red, yellow, and blue) plus black.

FOX - Abbreviation for **Foxing**.

FOXING - Defect caused by mold growth which results in a spotting effect usually at the edges of comic books.

FREEZE DRY - Process used to preserve wet paper before mildew damage can occur.

FUMETTI - Illustration system in which individual frames of a film are colored and used for individual panels to make a comic book story. The most famous example is DC's *Movie Comics* #1-6 from 1939.

GATEFOLD COVER - A double-width fold-out cover.

GENRE - Categories of comic book subject matter; e.g. Science Fiction, Super-Hero, Romance, Funny Animal, Teenage Humor, Crime, War, Western, Mystery, Horror, etc.

GIVEAWAY - Type of comic book intended to be given away as a premium or promotional device instead of being sold.

GLASSES ATTACHED - In 3-D comics, the special blue and red cellophane and cardboard glasses are still attached to the comic.

GLASSES DETACHED - In 3-D comics, the special blue and red cellophane and cardboard glasses are not still attached to the comic; obviously less desirable than **Glasses Attached**.

GLUE or GLUED - Restoration method in which some form of glue was used to repair or reinforce a comic book defect.

GOLDEN AGE - Comics published from approximately 1938 (*Action Comics* #1) to 1945.

GOOD GIRL ART - Refers to a style of art, usually from the 1930s-50s, that portrays women in a sexually implicit way.

GRADE or GRADING - That's what this whole book is about!

GREASE PENCIL - A wax-based marker commonly used to write on cardboard.

GREASE PENCIL ON COVER - Indicates that someone marked the cover of a comic with a grease pencil, usually with a resale price or an arrival date.

GREY-TONE COVER - A cover art style in which pencil or charcoal underlies the normal line drawing, used to enhance the effects of light and shadow, thus producing a richer quality. These covers, prized by most collectors, are sometimes referred to as **Painted Covers** but are not actually painted.

HB - Abbreviation for Hardback.

HEAVY CREASING - A crease that is longer than 2 inches.

HLP - Abbreviation for Hole Punched.

HOT STAMPING - The process of pressing foil, prism paper and/or inks on cover stock.

HRN - Abbreviation for Highest Reorder Number. This refers to a method used by collectors of Gilberton's *Classic Comics* and *Classics Illustrated* series to distinguish first editions from later printings.

IBC - Abbreviation for Inside Back Cover.

IFC - Abbreviation for Inside Front Cover.

ILLO - Abbreviation for Illustration.

IMPAINT - Another term for **Color Touch**.

INDICIA - Publishing and title information usually located at the bottom of the first page or the bottom of the inside front cover. In rare cases and in some pre-1938 comics, it was sometimes located on internal pages.

INFINITY COVER - Shows a scene that repeats itself to infinity.

INITIALS ON COVER - Someone's initials in pencil, pen, or grease pencil written on the cover.

INIT. ON CVR - Short for **Initials on Cover**.

INK SKIP - Printing defect in which the printing roller momentarily receives no ink, causing a streak or blank spot.

INK SMUDGE - Printing defect in which ink is smeared, usually by handling, before the ink is completely dry; these defects commonly look like fingerprints.

INTRO - Same as **Debut**.

INVESTMENT GRADE COPY - (1) Comic of sufficiently high grade and demand to be viewed by collectors as instantly liquid should the need arise to sell; (2) A comic in VF or better condition; (3) A comic purchased primarily to realize a profit.

ISSUE NUMBER - The actual edition number of a given title.

ISH - Short for Issue.

JAPAN PAPER - An archival paper used to repair tears and replace missing pieces when restoring a comic book.

JLA - Abbreviation for Justice League of America.

JOINED PAGES - (1) Bindery detect in which pages are "trimmed long" and are not separated at right hand corner(s) or along right edge. See **Siamese Pages**; (2) A rare printing defect where a new roll of paper is glued to the spent roll while still on the press. This glued intersection appears as a vertical stripe of double thick newsprint on one of the interior pages.

JSA - Abbreviations for Justice Society of America.

KEY, KEY BOOK or KEY ISSUE - An issue that contains a first appearance, origin, or other historically or artistically important feature considered especially desirable by collectors.

LAMINATED - Clear plastic with adhesive used by early collectors to protect comics; an outdated and destructive technique which virtually eliminates collector value.

LAMONT LARSON - Pedigreed collection of high grade 1940s comics with the initials or name of its original owner, Lamont Larson.

LATERAL BAR - See **Staple Lateral Bar**.

LBC - Abbreviation for Left [Side or Edge of] Back Cover.

LENTICULAR COVERS or "FLICKER" COVERS - A comic book cover overlayed with a ridged plastic sheet such that the special artwork underneath appears to move when the cover is tilted at different angles perpendicular to the ridges.

LETTER COL or LETTER COLUMN - A feature in a comic book that prints and sometimes responds to letters written by its readers.

LFC - Abbreviation for Left [Side or Edge of] Front Cover.

LFT - Abbreviation for Left. Not much of an abbreviation, is it?

LGC - Abbreviation for **Logo Cut**.

LIGHT CREASING - A crease 2" long or less.

LINE DRAWN COVER - A cover published in the traditional way where pencil sketches are overdrawn with india ink and then colored. See also **Grey-Tone Cover**, **Photo Cover**, and **Painted Cover**.

LLBC - Abbreviation for Lower Left [Corner of] Back Cover.

LLFC - Abbreviation for Lower Left [Corner of] Front Cover.

LOGO - The title of a strip or comic book as it appears on the cover or title page.

LOGO CUT - See **Remainders**.

LOOSE STAPLE - Staple that can be easily moved and no longer holds comic pages tightly. See **Popped Staple**.

LRBC - Abbreviation for Lower Right [Corner of] Back Cover.

LRFC - Abbreviation for Lower Right [Corner of] Front Cover.

LS - Abbreviation for **Loose Staple**.

LSH - Abbreviation for Legion of Super-Heroes.

LT - Abbreviation for Light.

MAGIC LIGHTNING COLLECTION - A collection of high grade 1950s comics from the San Francisco area.

MANUFACTURING FOLD - A defect in which some page(s) of the comic (usually the cover) is folded during the printing and/or the paper manufacturing process.

MARVEL CHIPPING - A bindery (trimming/cutting) defect that results in a series of chips and tears at the top, bottom, and right edges of the cover, caused when the cutting blade of an industrial paper trimmer becomes dull. It was dubbed Marvel Chipping because it can be found quite often on Marvel comics from the late '50s and early '60s but can also occur with any company's comic books from the late 1940s through the middle 1960s.

MAVERICK PAGES or MAVERICK SIGNATURE - Interior pages that are not the same size or shape as the rest of the interior; most commonly a bindery defect.

MAVERICK STAPLE - See **Deformed Staple**.

MID-SPINE - Between the staples.

MILE HIGH COLLECTION - High grade collection of over 22,000 comics discovered in Denver, Colorado in 1977, originally owned by Mr. Edgar Church. Comics from this collection are now famous for extremely white pages, fresh smell, and beautiful cover ink reflectivity.

MIN - Abbreviation for Minor.

MISCUT or MISTRIMMED - Bindery defect where cover and/or pages are not cut square or are cut to wrong size.

MISWRAPPED - Bindery defect where staple and fold do not intersect the center of the cover, causing some of the back cover to appear on the front of the comic or some of the front cover to ride around to the back.

MOD - Abbreviation for Moderate.

MODERN AGE - A catch-all term usually applied to comics published from the 1980s to the present.

MOISTURE DAMAGE - Wrinkling and/or stains caused by absorption of a liquid.

MOISTURE DAMAGE or MOISTURE RING - Wrinkling and/or stains, often circular, caused by absorption of moisture, often from the bottom of a cup or glass.

MOTH BALL SMELL - The aroma that infuses some comic books because of their storage with moth balls. Some comics from specific collections can be identified by this characteristic odor.

MS - Abbreviation for Missing Staple.

MULTIPLE BINDERY STAPLES - Bindery defect in which the comic book is stapled additional times unnecessarily.

MYLAR™ - An inert, very hard, space-age plastic used to make high quality protective bags and sleeves for comic book storage. "Mylar" is a trademark of the DuPont Co.

NAME STAMP - Indicates that an ink stamp with someone's name (and sometimes address) has been stamped in or on the comic book.

NBC - Abbreviation for No Back Cover.

NC - Abbreviation for No Cover.

ND - Abbreviation for No Date.

NFC - Abbreviation for No Front Cover.

NGL - Abbreviation for No (3-D) Glasses.

NIT-PICKER - Collector/investor who is never satisfied with the condition of a comic book, regardless of quality. But you're OK.

NN - Abbreviation for No Number.

NO COVER - Come on, do you really need a definition for this one? See **Coverless**...if you have to.

NO DATE - When there is no date given on the cover or indicia page.

NO NUMBER - No issue number is given on the cover or indicia page; these are usually first issues or one-shots.

NOC - Abbreviation for Name on Cover.

OFF-CENTER FOLDING - See **Folding Error**.

OFF-SET COVER - See **Folding Error**.

OIL DAMAGE or OIL STAIN - A defect in which oil has penetrated the cover and /or interior pages, causing them to become translucent in the area of the stain.

ONE-SHOT - When only one issue is published of a title, or when a series is published where each issue is a different title (e.g. Dell's *Four Color Comics*).

ORIGIN - When the story of a character's creation is given.

OS - Abbreviation for **Oxidation Shadow**.

OVER-COVER - A condition common in 1950s comic books where the cover extends approximately 1/16 of an inch beyond the interior pages. Because this margin is unsupported by the interior pages, it is more susceptible to damage.

O/W - Abbreviation for Otherwise.

OWL - Overstreet Whiteness Level, a scale for evaluating paper color established in the original *Overstreet Comic Book Grading Guide*.

OXIDATION SHADOW - Darker, usually linear area at the edge of some comics stored in stacks. Some portion of the cover was not covered by the comic immediately above it, and it was exposed to the air. Also see **Dust Shadow** and **Sun Shadow**.

PAGES MISSING - One or more pages have been removed from the comic.

PAGES OUT OF ORDER - A rare bindery defect in which the pages of a comic book are bound together in the wrong order.

PAGES TRIMMED - The top, bottom and right-hand edges of the comic (or possibly interior pages) have been trimmed with a paper cutter, hand blade, or pneumatic cutter to hide edge defects.

PAGES UPSIDE DOWN - A rare bindery defect in which the cover orientation is reversed relative to the orientation of the interior pages.

PAINTED COVER - (1) Cover taken from an actual painting instead of a line drawing; (2) Inaccurate name for a grey-toned cover.

PANELOLOGIST - One who researches comic books and/or comic strips.

PANNAPICTAGRAPHIST - One possible term for someone who collects comic books; can you figure out why it hasn't exactly taken off in common parlance?

PAPER ABRASION - Rough patch or area where the paper has been abraded on a rough surface, leaving a rough texture that is often faded.

PAPER COVER - Comic book cover made from the same newsprint as the interior pages. These books are extremely rare in high grade.

PARADE OF PLEASURE - A book about the censorship of comics.

PB - Abbreviation for Paperback.

PC - Abbreviation for Piece.

PEDIGREE - A book from a famous and usually high grade collection - e.g. Allentown, Lamont Larson, Edgar Church/Mile High, Denver, San Francisco, Cosmic Aeroplane, etc. Beware of non-pedigree collections being promoted as pedigree books; only outstanding high grade collections similar to those listed qualify.

PERFECT BINDING - Pages are glued to the cover as opposed to being stapled to the cover, resulting in a flat binded side. Also known as **Square Back or Square Bound**.

PERFORATIONS - Small holes at the page margins which sometimes occur as part of the manufacturing process; not considered a defect. Perforations are sometimes used to tell if a comic is an unread copy. In such a copy, tell-tale clicks are heard when the book is opened for the first time as the perforations separate.

PG - Abbreviation for Page.

PHOTO COVER - Comic book cover featuring a photographic image instead of a line drawing or painting.

PHOTO-REACTIVE COLORS or INKS - Certain inks used in the printing of comics that contain a higher proportion of metals, thus decreasing their stability and resistance to fading; comics with these inks/colors commonly have faded covers. Examples are: "DC dark green" (e.g. *Showcase* #8, *Superman* #100), blue (*Showcase* #13), purple (*Showcase* #14), and orange-red (*Showcase* #4).

PICKLE SMELL - A colloquial description of the odor of acetic acid, often associated with browning and/or brittle paper. See **Vinegar Smell**.

PICTORIAL COVER - Another term for **Photo Cover**.

PIN HOLES - Tiny holes often passing through the covers and multiple pages of a comic where a pin was used to tack the comic to a board. In some cases, the paper displaced by the pin may still be present but frayed; in other cases, removal of the pin may have torn away miniscule pieces of paper around the hole.

PLATINUM AGE - Comics published from approximately 1900-1938.

PNEUMATIC CUTTER - An industrial tool used to shear large amounts of paper.

PNL - Abbreviation for Panel.

POC - Abbreviation for Pencil On Cover.

POLYPROPALENE - A type of plastic used in the manufacture of comic book bags; now considered harmful to paper and not recommended for long term storage of comics.

POOO - Abbreviation for **Pages Out Of Order.**

POP - Abbreviation for the anti-comic book volume, *Parade of Pleasure.*

POPPED STAPLE - A term used to describe a condition where the cover has split at the staple and has become detached or popped loose. See **Loose Staple.**

POST-CODE - Describes comics published after February 1955 and usually displaying the CCA stamp in the upper right-hand corner.

POUGHKEEPSIE - Refers to a large collection of Dell Comics file copies believed to have originated from the warehouse of Western Publishing in Poughkeepsie, NY.

PP - Abbreviation for Pages.

PRE-CODE - Describes comics published before the **Comics Code Authority** seal began appearing on covers in 1955.

PRE-HERO DC - A term used to describe *More Fun* #1-51 (pre-Spectre), *Adventure* #1-39 (pre-Sandman), and *Detective* #1-26 (pre-Batman). The term is actually inaccurate because technically there were "heroes" in the above books.

PRE-HERO MARVEL - A term used to describe *Strange Tales* #1-100 (pre-Human Torch), *Journey Into Mystery* #1-82 (pre-Thor), *Tales To Astonish* #1-35 (pre-Ant Man), and *Tales Of Suspense* #1-38 (pre-Iron Man).

PRICE STICKERS - Adhesive stickers applied to comic covers to alter the cover price; often considered a defect.

PRINTERS' SMUDGE - See **Ink Smudge.**

PRINTING DEFECT - A defect caused by the printing process. Examples would include paper wrinkling, miscut edges, misfolded spine, untrimmed pages, off-registered color, off-centered trimming, misfolded and unbound pages. It should be noted that these are all defects that lower the grade of the book.

PRINT-THROUGH - The printing on the inside of the front cover is visible (to varying degrees) from the front cover as if one were looking through the front cover. This is not always considered a defect. See **Transparent Cover.**

PROGRESSIVE ROLLED SPINE - A spine roll that is more pronounced on one end than the other.

PROVENANCE - When the owner of a book is known and is stated for the purpose of authenticating and documenting the history of the book. Example: A book from the Stan Lee or Forrest Ackerman collection would be an example of a value-adding provenance.

PULP - Cheaply produced magazine made from low grade newsprint. The term comes from the wood pulp that was used in the paper manufacturing process.

PUZZLE FILLED IN - Game or puzzle inside a comic book that has been written on, thus reducing the value of the comic.

QUARTERLY - Published every three months (four times a year).

QUINONE - (1) The substance in ink that promotes oxidation and discoloration and is associated with transfer stains; (2) A yellowish, crystalline compound with an irritating odor, obtained by the oxidation of aniline, and regarded as a benzene with two hydrogen atoms replaced by two oxygen atoms. It is used in tanning and making dyes. Quinone will oxidize another material and itself reduce to hydroquinone. Bet you wished you paid attention in chemistry class now. See **Aniline.**

R - Abbreviation for Reprint.

RARE - 10-20 copies estimated to exist.

RAT CHEW - Damage caused by the gnawing of rats and mice.

RBC - Abbreviation for Right [Side or Edge of] Back Cover.

RBCC - Abbreviation for Rockets Blast Comic Collector, one of the first and most prominent adzines instrumental in developing the early comic book market.

READING COPY - A comic that is in FAIR to GOOD condition and is often used for research; the condition has been sufficiently reduced to the point where general handling will not degrade it further.

READING CREASE - Book-length, vertical front cover crease at staples, caused by bending the cover over the staples. Square-bounds receive these creases just by opening the cover too far to the left.

RECESSED STAPLES - When the staple lateral bar penetrates below the plane of the cover without breaking through.

REGLOSSING - A repair technique where silicone or other clear sprays are applied to comic book covers in an attempt to restore cover ink reflectivity. This is not generally viewed as an ethical practice and therefore reduces the value of the comic.

REMAINDERS - Comic books that remain unsold at the newsstand. In the past, the top 1/4 to 1/3 of the cover (or in some cases the entire cover) was removed and returned to the publisher for credit; this is the reason many comics from 1936-1965 are sometimes found as **Coverless, Three-Fourths,** or **Two-Thirds** cover copies.

REPRINT COMICS - In earlier decades, comic books that contained newspaper strip reprints; modern reprint comics usually contain stories originally featured in older comic books.

RES - Abbreviation for Restored.

RESEARCH COPY - See **Reading Copy.**

RESTORATION - Any attempt, whether professional or amateur, to enhance the appearance of an aging or damaged comic book. These procedures may include any or all of the following techniques: recoloring, adding missing paper, stain, ink, dirt or tape removal, whitening, pressing out wrinkles, staple replacement, trimming, re-glossing, etc. Amateur work can lower the value of a book, and even professional restoration has now gained a certain negative aura in the modern marketplace from some quarters. In all cases, except for some simple cleaning procedures, a restored book can never be worth the same as an unrestored book in the same condition.

RESTORED COPY - A comic book that has had restoration work.

RETURN or RETURN COPY - See **Remainders.**

REVIVAL - An issue that begins republishing a comic book character after a period of dormancy.

RFC - Abbreviation for Right [Side or Edge of] Front Cover.

RICE PAPER - A thin, transparent paper commonly used by restorers to repair tears and replace small pieces on covers and pages of comic books. Also see **Japan Paper.**

RIP - An uneven rough tear; different from a split or cut.

RLS - Abbreviation for **Rolled Spine.**

ROLLED SPINE - A condition where the left edge of a comic book curves toward the front or back; a defect caused by folding back each page as the comic was read. See **Progressive Rolled Spine.**

ROUGH SPINE - See **Abraded Spine.**

ROUND BOUND - Standard saddle stitch binding typical of most comics.

ROUNDED CORNER - See **Abraded Corner.**

RT - Abbreviation for Right.

RUN - A group of comics of one title where most or all of the issues are present. See **Complete Run.**

RUST MIGRATION - Rust stains that have moved from the staples to the adjacent paper.

RUST STAIN - (1) A red-brown stain caused by proximity to a rusty object; (2) A stain associated with rusty staples. This is considered a defect.

RUSTY STAPLES - Staples that have oxidized through exposure to moisture in the air.

SADDLE STITCH - The staple binding of magazines and comic books.

SC - Abbreviation for **Subscription Crease**.

SCARCE - 20-100 copies estimated to exist.

SCRAPED STAPLE - A staple which has had rust or other discoloration removed by scraping the surface. This condition is readily identifiable under a hand lens or magnifying glass.

SCUFF or PAPER SCUFF - A light paper abrasion.

SEDUCTION OF THE INNOCENT - An inflammatory book written by Dr. Frederic Wertham and published in 1953; Wertham asserted that comics were responsible for rampant juvenile deliquency in American youth.

SET - (1) A complete run of a given title; (2) A grouping of comics for sale.

SEMI-MONTHLY - Published twice a month, but not necessarily **Bi-Weekly**.

SEWN SPINE - A comic with many spine perforations where binders' thread held it into a bound volume. This is considered a defect.

SF - Abbreviation for Science Fiction (the other commonly used term, "sci-fi," is often considered derogatory or indicative of more "low-brow" rather than "literary" science fiction, i.e. "sci-fi television."

SHALLOW STAPLE - A staple that has not penetrated all of the pages and is not visible at the centerfold. See **Deformed Staple**.

SIAMESE PAGES - A bindery defect in which pages are "trimmed long" and are not separated at right-hand corner(s) or along right edge. See **Joined Pages**.

SIGNATURE or SIG - A large sheet of paper printed with four, or a multiple of four, pages. When folded, it becomes a section of one comic book.

SIGNATURE DUPLICATED - A rare bindery defect in which a signature is inadvertently duplicated. This may also displace and/or replace an adjacent signature.

SIGNATURE OUT OF ORDER - A rare bindery defect in which signatures are bound in the wrong sequence. For example, a 32-page comic book with this defect usually has pages in the following order: 9-16, 1-8, 25-32, 17-24.

SIGNATURE REVERSED - A rare bindery defect in which the orientation of one of the signatures is reversed and appears upside down and backwards.

SILVER AGE - Comics published from approximately 1956 (*Showcase* #4) to 1969.

SILVER PROOF - A black and white actual size print on thick glossy paper hand-painted by an artist to indicate colors to the engraver.

SIZING - The glaze applied to newsprint at the end of the manufacturing process.

SLAB - Colloquial term for the plastic enclosure used by grading certification companies to seal in certified comics.

SLABBING - Colloquial term for the process of encapsulating certified comics in a plastic enclosure.

SLICK COVER - Any cover that is made from clay-coated paper stock.

SLT - Abbreviation for Slight.

SM - Abbreviation for Small.

SMOKE DAMAGE - Grey or black discoloration caused by smoke. This is considered a defect.

SOILING - Organic and inorganic substances and residues on the surface of the paper; different from stains, smudges, and mildew.

SOTI - Abbreviation for **Seduction of the Innocent**.

SPINE - The left-hand edge of the comic that has been folded and stapled.

SPINE CHIP - A small piece missing from the area of the spine.

SPINE ROLL - See **Rolled Spine** and **Progressive Rolled Spine**.

SPINE SPLIT - An even separation at the spine fold, commonly above or below the staple.

SPINE STRESS - A small fold, usually less than 1/4 inch long, perpendicular to the spine.

SPL - Abbreviation for **Spine Split**.

SPLASH PAGE - A **Splash Panel** that takes up the entire page.

SPLASH PANEL - (1) The first panel of a comic book story, usually larger than other panels and usually containing the title and credits of the story; (2) An oversized interior panel.

SPLIT SPINE - See **Spine Split**.

SPN - Abbreviation for **Spine**.

SQUARE BACK or SQUARE BOUND - See **Perfect Binding**.

SS - Abbreviation for **Store Stamp**.

STAINS - Discoloration caused by a foreign substance.

STAMP PAGE - Page devoted to the sale and discussion of stamp collecting; common in comics of the 1930s.

STAPLE EXTENDERS - The portion of the staple that actually penetrates the paper and can be seen at the centerfold; the portion of the staple that is bent either upwards or downwards toward the center of the staple.

STAPLE HOLE - A punched-out area in cover and interior pages caused by staple extender. This hole becomes enlarged (abraded) when staples are removed and replaced several times.

STAPLE LATERAL BAR - The portion of the staple that does not penetrate the paper and lies on top of the cover parallel to the spine; the part of the staple visible on the outside of the comic.

STAPLE PAGE - Term used by early collectors to describe the **Centerfold**.

STAPLE REINFORCED - (1) To strengthen with additional materials the cover paper at the site of staple contact; (2) To strengthen with additional materials the centerfold and/or other pages at the points of staple contact.

STAPLE RUST MIGRATION - Rust stains have moved from the staple to the paper.

STAPLE TEAR - Most often indicates paper separation at the staple.

STAPLE POPPED - Staple tear; staple has "popped" loose from the cover.

STICKER ON COVER - Price, name, or other sticker adhered to cover.

STN - Abbreviation for **Staining**.

STORE STAMP - Store name (and sometimes address and telephone number) stamped in ink via rubber stamp and stamp pad.

STP - Abbreviation for **Staples**.

STRESS LINES - Light, tiny wrinkles occuring along the spine, projecting from the staples or appearing anywhere on the covers of a comic book.

STRESS SPLIT - Any clean paper separation caused by pressure; most common at the spine.

SUBSCRIPTION COPY - A comic sent through the mail directly from the publisher or publisher's agent. Most are folded in half, causing a subscription crease or fold running down the center of the comic from top to bottom; this is considered a defect.

SUBSCRIPTION CREASE - See **Subscription Copy**.

SUBSCRIPTION FOLD - See **Subscription Copy**. Differs from a **Subscription Crease** in that no ink is missing as a result of the fold.

SUN - Abbreviation for **Sun Shadow**.

SUN SHADOW - Darker, usually linear area at the edge of some comics stored in stacks. Some portion of the cover was not covered by the comic immediately above it, and it suffered prolonged exposure to light. A serious defect, unlike a **Dust Shadow**, which can sometimes be removed. Also see **Oxidation Shadow**.

SUPER-HERO - A costumed crime fighter with powers beyond those of mortal man.

SUPER-VILLAIN - A costumed criminal with powers beyond those of mortal man; the antithesis of Super-Hero.

SUPPLE - The condition of paper with little or no deterioration. This kind of paper is bendable, pliant, and limber; the other end of the spectrum from **Brittleness**.

SWIPE - A panel, sequence, or story obviously borrowed from previously published material.

TANNIN LINE - A brownish stain line of tannin that occurs when wet comic book paper dries.

TAPE RESIDUE - Adhesive substance from cellophane tape which has penetrated paper fibers.

TAPE PULL - Loss of artwork or color when a piece of tape stuck to the cover has been improperly removed from the paper surface.

TAPE STAIN - See **Tape Residue**.

TEAR - An irregular separation of the paper; different from a split or cut.

TEAR SEALED - A tear that has been glued together.

TEXT ILLO. - A drawing or small panel in a text story that almost never has a dialogue balloon.

TEXT PAGE - A page with no panels or drawings.

TEXT STORY - A story with few if any illustrations commonly used as filler material during the first three decades of comics.

3-D COMIC - Comic art that is drawn and printed in two color layers, producing a 3-D effect when viewed through special glasses.

3-D EFFECT COMIC - Comic art that is drawn to appear as if in 3-D but isn't.

THREE-FOURTHS COVER - See **Remainders**.

TITLE - The name of the comic book.

TITLE PAGE - First page of a story showing the title of the story and possibly the creative credits and indicia.

TOBC - Abbreviation for Top Of Back Cover.

TOFC - Abbreviation for Top Of Front Cover.

TOS - (1) Abbreviation for Tape On Spine; (2) Abbreviation for *Tales of Suspense*.

TP - Abbreviation for **Tape Pull**.

TR - Abbreviation for **Tear**.

TRANSFER STAIN - Ink from the first page rubs off onto the inside front cover, causing certain portions to appear yellowed; often mistaken for paper deterioration. Can also occur on inside back cover.

TRANSPARENT COVER - The printing on the inside front cover is visible (to varying degrees) from the outside front cover. This is not always considered a defect. See **Print-Through**.

TRIMMED - (1) A bindery process which separates top, right, and bottom of pages and cuts comic books to the proper size; (2) A repair process in which defects along the edges of a comic book are removed with the use of scissors, razor blades, and/or paper cutters. Comic books which have been repaired in this fashion are considered defectives.

TTA - Abbreviation for *Tales to Astonish*.

TWO-THIRDS COVER - See **Remainders**.

UK - Abbreviation for British edition (United Kingdom).

ULBC - Abbreviation for Upper Left Corner Of Back Cover.

ULFC - Abbreviation for Upper Left Corner Of Front Cover.

UPGRADE - To obtain another copy of the same comic book in a higher grade.

URBC - Abbreviation for Upper Right Corner Of Back Cover.

URFC - Abbreviation for Upper Right Corner Of Front Cover.

VARIANT COVER - A different cover image used on the same issue.

VERY RARE - 1 to 10 copies estimated to exist.

VICTORIAN AGE - Comics published from approximately 1828-1899.

VINEGAR SMELL - The smell of acetic acid in newsprint that is deteriorating.

WANT LIST - A listing of comics needed by a collector, or a list of comics that a collector is interested in purchasing.

WAREHOUSE COPY - Originating from a publisher's warehouse; similar to file copy.

WATER DAMAGE - See **Moisture Damage**.

WC - Abbreviation for **White Cover**.

WD - Abbreviation for **Water Damage**.

WHITE COVER - A comic cover where white is the predominant color. These covers are easily stained and/or damaged and readily show wear. Because they rarely occur in high grade, white covers are in great demand by collectors.

WHITE MOUNTAIN COLLECTION - A collection of high grade 1950s and 1960s comics which originated in New England.

WHITE PAGES - A term used to describe interior pages in the best state of preservation; the preferred state of interior pages.

WHITENESS LEVEL - The whiteness of interior pages compared against a whiteness standard like the OWL scale.

WOC - Abbreviation for Writing On Cover.

WORM HOLE - Small holes eaten into paper caused by a variety of insects and boring worms...not a deformation in space-time that leads to the Gamma Quadrant. Most worm hole damage is actually caused by termites, not Jem'Hadar soldiers.

WP - Abbreviation for **White Pages**.

WR - Abbreviation for **Writing**.

WRAP - A single sheet of paper folded to form four pages of story (counting both sides) and bound into a comic; the centerfold is a wrap, as is the cover and all successive pages. The "first" or "outer" wrap is the first interior page after the cover.

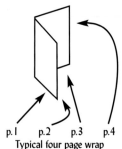

Typical four page wrap

WRP - Abbreviation for **Wrap**.

WRONG COVER - A rare bindery defect in which the cover from one comic is stapled to the interior pages of another comic.

WS - Abbreviation for Water Stain.

X-OVER - Short for **Crossover**.

YEL - Abbreviation for Yellowing.

ZINE - Short for **Fanzine**.

Advertisers' Index

Overstreet Advisors

DAVID T. ALEXANDER
David Alexander Comics
Tampa, FL

DAVE ANDERSON
Want List Comics
Tulsa, OK

STEPHEN BARRINGTON
Collector
Chickasaw, AL

ROBERT BEERBOHM
Robert Beerbohm Comic Art
Fremont, NE

JON BERK
Collector
Hartford, CT

STEVE BOROCK
Primary Grader
Comics Guaranty, LLC

MICHAEL BROWNING
Collector
Jefferson City, TN

MICHAEL CARBONARO
Neatstuffcollectibles.com
Englewood, NJ

ERICK CARTER
Tropic Comics
Plantation, FL

GARY CARTER
Collector
Coronado, CA

JOHN CHRUSCINSKI
Tropic Comics
Plantation, FL

GARY COLABUONO
Classics International Ent.
Elk Grove Village, IL

BILL COLE
Bill Cole Enterprises, Inc.
Randolph, MA

LARRY CURCIO
Avalon Comics
Los Angeles, CA

GARY DOLGOFF
Gary Dolgoff Comics
Easthampton, MA

BRUCE ELLSWORTH
Neatstuffcollectibles.com
Dallas, TX

CONRAD ESCHENBERG
Collector/Dealer
Cold Spring, NY

RICHARD EVANS
Bedrock City Comics
Houston, TX

STEPHEN FISHLER
Metropolis Collectibles, Inc.
New York, NY

DAN FOGEL
Hippy Comix, Inc.
El Sobrante, CA

STEVEN GENTNER
Golden Age Specialist
Portland, OR

STEVE GEPPI
Diamond Int. Galleries
Timonium, MD

MICHAEL GOLDMAN
Motor City Comics
Southfield, MI

TOM GORDON
Monumental Collectibles
Westminster, MD

JAMIE GRAHAM
Graham Crackers
Chicago, IL

DANIEL GREENHALGH
Showcase New England
Northford, CT

ERIC J. GROVES
Dealer/Collector
Oklahoma City, OK

ROBERT HALL
Collector
Harrisburg, PA

JIM HALPERIN
Heritage Comics Auctions
Dallas, TX

BRUCE HAMILTON
Collector
Prescott, AZ

MARK HASPEL
Grader
Comics Guaranty, LLC

JOHN HAUSER
Dealer/Collector
New Berlin, WI

BILL HUGHES
Dealer/Collector
Flower Mound, TX

ROB HUGHES
Arch Angels
Manhattan Beach, CA

ED JASTER
Heritage Comics Auctions
Dallas, TX

JOSHUA NATHANSON
ComicLink
Little Neck, NY

TODD REZNIK
Pacific Comic Exchange
Palos Verdes Peninsula, CA

JOHN SNYDER
Diamond Int. Galleries
Timonium, MD

PHIL LEVINE
Dealer/Collector
Three Bridges, NJ

MATT NELSON
Classic Conservations
New Orleans, LA

ROBERT ROGOVIN
Four Color Comics
New York, NY

TONY STARKS
Silver Age Specialist
Evansville, IN

PATRICK MARCHBANKS
Golden Age Comics & Games
Gulfport, MS

RICHARD OLSON
Collector/Academician
Slidell, LA

RORY ROOT
Comic Relief
Berkeley, CA

TERRY STROUD
Dealer/Collector
Santa Monica, CA

HARRY MATETSKY
Collector
Middletown, NJ

TERRY O'NEILL
Terry's Comics
Orange, CA

MARNIN ROSENBERG
Collectors Assemble
Great Neck, NY

DOUG SULIPA
"Everything 1960-1996"
Manitoba, Canada

JON McCLURE
Dealer/Collector
Newport, OR

JIM PAYETTE
Golden Age Specialist
Bethlehem, NH

ROBERT ROTER
Pacific Comic Exchange
Palos Verdes Peninsula, CA

MICHAEL TIERNEY
The Comic Book Store
Little Rock, AR

MIKE McKENZIE
Alternate Worlds
Cockeysville, MD

CHRIS PEDRIN
Pedrin Conservatory
Redwood City, CA

CHUCK ROZANSKI
Mile High Comics
Denver, CO

JOE VERENEAULT
JHV Associates
Woodbury Heights, NJ

PETER MEROLO
Collector
Sedona, AZ

JOHN PETTY
Heritage Comics Auctions
Dallas, TX

MATT SCHIFFMAN
Bronze Age Specialist
Aloha, OR

JERRY WEIST
Collector
Gloucester, MA

DALE MOORE
Quality Control
Comics Guaranty, LLC

JIM PITTS
Hippy Comix, Inc.
El Sobrante, CA

DAVID SINCERE
Sincere Comics
Mobile, AL

HARLEY YEE
Dealer/Collector
Detroit, MI

MICHAEL NAIMAN
Silver Age Specialist
San Diego, CA

RON PUSSELL
Redbeard's Book Den
Crystal Bay, NV

DAVID SMITH
Fantasy Illustrated/Rocket Comics
Seattle, WA

VINCENT ZURZOLO, JR.
Metropolis Collectibles, Inc.
New York, NY